a Haircut in Horse Town...

and Other Great Car Talk Puzzlers

Tom and Ray Magliozzi
aka Click and Clack,
The Tappet Brothers
with Doug Berman

A Haircut in Horsetown... is produced by becker&mayer!, Kirkland, WA.
www.beckermayer.com

Edited by Lissa Wolfendale
Design by Sullivan Scully Design Group
Art direction by Simon Sung
Production by Vincent Enche
Photo manipulation by Mike Erter

ISBN: 1-892353-00-8
10 9 8 7 6 5 4 3 2 1

Visit us at the Car Talk section of cars.com.

Table of Contents

Introduction

The puzzler has been at the center of "Car Talk" from almost the very beginning. You may think of it as a conundrum; a carefully constructed brain teaser designed to keep your mind agile and amused during the week ahead. You may think of it that way. But not us. We think of it as a way to kill time during the show. An hour's an awfully long time to sit there and pretend you know what you're talking about!

When Ray first came up with the idea for "the puzzler," we were thrilled. We jumped up and down and patted him on the back and gave him high-fives. "Way to go, Ray," we said. "The puzzler's a great idea! Bring one every week."

And for a while, everything went beautifully. At the designated time, Ray would launch into his new puzzler. Tom would listen, interrupt, cajole, and Ray would obfuscate. And before the guys knew it, five minutes would be gone. "Whoopie!" we said. Miraculously, the audience seemed to genuinely enjoy the puzzler, too (judging by the diminishing amount of hate mail we received).

But then one day, Ray came in all bleary-eyed. "What's wrong?" Tom asked. "I've been up for two days," admits Ray. "I'm all out of puzzlers."

That was about nineteen years ago. So we quickly turned to the most logical and elegant solution we could think of: theft. We stole puzzlers from everybody. From our friends, family members, listeners, colleagues, customers, librarians, bums in Hahvahd Squayah, and especially from the greatest puzzle master of them all, Martin Gardner, puzzle editor emeritus of *Scientific American*.

We knew we were safe from copyright laws, because a learned man like Martin Gardner would never waste his time listening to a show like ours. And when we finally heard that the great Martin Gardner had passed away, we figured it was safe to go into print! As we explained to our listeners recently, "Since that old geezer, Martin Gardner is dead, how's he going to sue us now?"

Well, to our great surprise, we received an urgent piece of correspondence from Martin Gardner's son, Jim, telling us that the grand old puzzle master was not only still alive and kicking, but lucid, too! We didn't believe him, so we called Martin ourselves. The conversation went something like this:

"Hello?"

"Is this Martin Gardner?"

"Yes."

"Are you dead?"

"No." (Hangs up.)

So given the circumstances, our lawyers have suggested that we dedicate this first volume of *Great Car Talk Puzzlers* to Martin Gardner. He is, after all, the world's most recognized puzzle master, and was our inspiration for introducing the puzzler on our show in the first place. And if you're still around whenever we get around to publishing *Volume II*, Martin, I believe the out-of-court settlement requires us to dedicate that one to you, too.

Enjoy.

Doug Berman
Esteemed Producer
Car Talk

How We Create the Puzzlers: Perception versus Reality

Over the years a bit of a disagreement has arisen over important aspects of the puzzler. We'd like to take a moment to dispel any confusion there might be by pointing out the perception...and the reality...of how the puzzler comes to you each week.

Selecting the Puzzler

Perception:

At our Los Alamos Puzzler Facility, teams of highly organized geniuses work late into the night, combing resources from all over the globe to craft quality puzzlers.

Reality:

Most of our puzzlers come from "Car Talk" staff member, Zuzu, who Doug Berman trained to type when she was a puppy.

Testing the Puzzler

Perception:

High level conferences are held each morning at Car Talk Plaza, assessing the relative strengths and weaknesses of each puzzler.

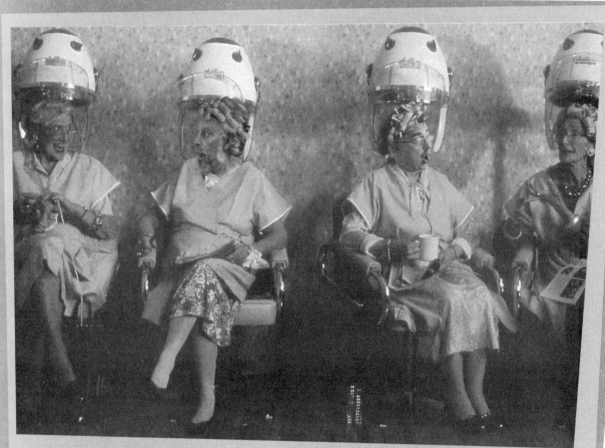

Reality:

Marge and Verna look over the puzzler every Tuesday morning at Mr. Gigi's. If they like it, we like it.

Choosing the Winner

Perception:

Our state-of-the-art CarTalkTronic 2000 reads and sorts thousands of incoming letters and e-mails. Cross-referencing zip codes and addresses, the main frame screens out duplicate submissions and answers submitted by NPR staff members (and the occasional Martin Gardner response). After processing all of this information, it randomly selects one winning entry and simultaneously notifies the IRS and NPR member stations.

Reality:
We pick the winner off the pile on Berman's desk.

Protesting the Answer

Perception:

Members of our civic-minded audience (like Edna Harriet Currier, shown here) take time out to compose thoughtful prose, addressing possible errors or inconsistencies in our puzzler presentation.

Reality:

Angry listeners stake out strategic positions along our route to Car Talk Plaza. Here, thanks again to the Governor, we are safely escorted to do another show by the always friendly Massachusetts National Guard.

The Official Puzzler Legend

 These puzzlers require right-brain, creative thinking.

 It's a mystery, so examine the clues closely.

 These puzzlers require left-brain, analytical thinking.

 Must be true, yet the answer still smells fishy.

 Automotive-related question.

 Danger! High degree of difficulty! Puzzler may cause you to pass a brain stone.

 You'll feel like a bonehead if you don't figure this one out!

 Historic. May require long-term memory or half-decent education.

 Requires math skills.

 Folkloric. Involves legends, lore, and stuff that fathers make up and pass off to their kids as true.

 Employs scientific principles!

The Tibetan Monk

RAY: This is a puzzler about a Tibetan monk.

TOM: Named Bubba?

RAY: No, not "Bubba." Baba. If he was from South Tibet, he would have been named Bubba. Now, Baba is planning to climb Tibet's holiest mountain to see the High Lama, who we'll call Roger Smith.

TOM: The same Roger Smith who ran General Motors?

RAY: Different Roger Smith. Anyway, Baba has to climb the mountain, and he does the journey in the following way: He leaves from the bottom of the mountain at 6:00 a.m.

TOM: Is that TST: Tibetan Standard Time?

RAY: Yes. Baba leaves at 6:00 a.m. TST, and he must reach the top by 6:00 p.m., twelve hours later. You got that? There is only one trail, and he must not leave the trail—not even to take a haircut.

TOM: Besides, if he left the trail, he'd what? Fall 12,000 feet into a gorge. If you leave the trail in Tibet, you're pretty much done for. Ask any yak.

RAY: Baba leaves at 6:00 a.m. and travels at varying speeds. He doesn't stray from the trail and he doesn't go backwards. He stops along the way to meditate, recite his mantra, read a few pages of Lao-tzu, play with his Game Boy, and so on. At 6:00 p.m. Baba gets there and finds the High Lama.

TOM: And he says, "Hi, Lama!"

RAY: Baba spends the night. The next morning at 6:00 a.m., Baba begins his descent of the mountain, which he does in the same fashion: stopping along the way, looking at the beautiful flowers, watching his step, and not deviating from the path. He goes fast, he goes slow, he does all kinds of things, and at 6:00 p.m. he reaches the bottom.

The question is: Is there any one point along the trail at which he finds himself at exactly the same time on both days? In other words, is there any time that he is at the exactly same spot that he was at—at that time—yesterday?

TOM: Isn't there a tram up this mountain? Does he really have to trek?

RAY: He's a monk. Trekking is in his job description.

TOM: A man's got to do what a man's got to do.

#1

Puzzler Answer:

TOM: This was an awesome puzzler.

RAY: It almost makes me want to invoke deep mathematical theories here, like the mean value theorem.

TOM: Or, maybe the Tibetan Uncertainty Principle? Beats me.

RAY: Actually, this puzzler is all about certainty, not uncertainty. Is there any time when Baba the monk would be at the same spot on both days?

TOM: There certainly is!

RAY: Not only is there any chance, there is a 100 percent certainty that one point will be coincident.

TOM: That's right. And the easiest way to think about it—heck, the only way to think about it— is this: What if Baba were twins, and at the very moment that he started out at the bottom of the mountain, his twin started out at the top of the mountain. Then what?

RAY: They must cross paths. There is only one trail, and they're both on it.

TOM: We don't know where, but there's got to be a point at which they're at the same point at the same time.

RAY: Interestingly enough, there's one point, and only one point. They can't cross more than what?

TOM: Once.

RAY: Very good, Tommy.

Ka-boom, Ka-boom

RAY: Vinny Goombatz decided to do a tune-up on his brother Vinny's car.

TOM: You mean, his other brother Vinny.

RAY: Of course. This tune-up included changing the spark plugs. Now, Vinny knew he had to be very careful not to allow any dirt to fall into the spark plug holes, where it might scratch the cylinder walls. If that happened, his brother would probably break his legs—again.

Vinny has a brainstorm and gets a great idea. After he removes the spark plugs, he decides to vacuum the dirt away from the spark plug holes with his official Click and Clack autographed model shop vac. He does this, and the results are, to say the least, disastrous.

TOM: Or at least exciting.

RAY: Very, very exciting. What happened?

Ray "adjusts" the intake of a '67 Cadillac Deville to fit a '91 Nissan Sentra.

#2

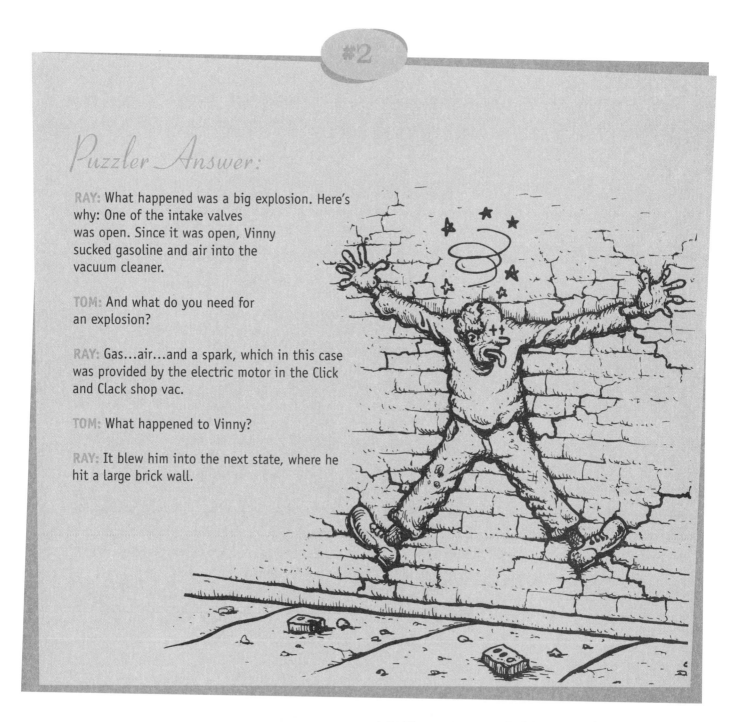

Puzzler Answer:

RAY: What happened was a big explosion. Here's why: One of the intake valves was open. Since it was open, Vinny sucked gasoline and air into the vacuum cleaner.

TOM: And what do you need for an explosion?

RAY: Gas...air...and a spark, which in this case was provided by the electric motor in the Click and Clack shop vac.

TOM: What happened to Vinny?

RAY: It blew him into the next state, where he hit a large brick wall.

Puzzler 3

How Tom's Car Got to Be a "Jalopy"

RAY: Everybody listening to "Car Talk" knows about jalopies—that is, broken-down cars with far too many miles on them.

TOM: Like, hypothetically speaking, '63 Dodge Darts.

RAY: Right. Hypothetically speaking. But have you ever wondered why a jalopy is called a jalopy?

TOM: No.

RAY: Well, start wondering, will you? What is the derivation of the word "jalopy" ?

#3

Puzzler Answer:

RAY: To answer this question, you have to go back to the 1920s, when large numbers of worn-out, old American cars were shipped to Mexico through the port of Vera Cruz. They were then transported inland to a town where they were remanufactured, and rehabilitated for sale throughout Mexico.

TOM: Do you mean to say, if you had a 1913 Stevens-Duryea and it got shipped to Mexico, it would be sold there as a remanufactured car?

RAY: Right. Out of five cars, they might make two. What was left over would then be shipped to New Jersey, for all we know, where the parts were probably used as temporary housing.

Before they got picked up by NPR, Tom and Ray used to do the show from Tom's front lawn.

#3

Anyway, the town to where they would get shipped was already famous for a certain very spicy type of pepper—jalapeño peppers—and the town is called Jalapa.

TOM: Jalapa. I love it!

RAY: The story goes that the longshoremen who were putting these junkers on the boats didn't know that the correct Mexican pronunciation for the town was "Ha-la-pa." So you know what they did?

TOM: They Americanized it and pronounced it "Ja-la-pa"?

RAY: Right, as in, "Hey, Rocky, we got us another one of these jalapas."

TOM: Sooner or later it turned into just plain old "jalopy."

RAY: Like your Dart.

 Vinnie's Intuition

RAY: This puzzler came to us from a high school student who listens to our show. Here's the letter he wrote:

Dear Tom and Ray,

It was a cold and blustery day. I was seated with Vinnie, the owner of Vinnie's Towing and Repair. We were drinking the first coffee of the day and were halfway through the first dozen donuts. Vinnie gazed out the window of his shop at the cars lined up at the light.

My school newspaper was running a feature on successful businessmen of the small town located between two ridges of mountains. I had been assigned to interview Vinnie, who was highly regarded in town. In fact, he was so good at spotting problems that some thought he was clairvoyant.

"Why are you so good at your job?" I asked.

"I just observe," Vinnie replied, as he continued to look out the window. I was worried about how to make this interview a success. How could I make him seem interesting? How did I get stuck with such a grunt?

"Take that car there, the one with the out-of-state plates," he said. "Notice that the people in the front seat are shivering and wiping the inside of the window with tissues as they're waiting for the light. You can see the vapor coming from their breath."

So what? I thought. *It's cold out!*

He watched the car pull through the intersection. "Let's go," he said.

"Where?" I asked, as we ran out for the wrecker.

"They'll break down before they get to the top of the mountain," replied Vinnie.

So we followed the car out of town on the main road, and sure enough, there they were at the side of the road, standing around with the hood up.

Here's the question: Can you guys guess what Vinnie saw at the intersection that indicated that the car was going to break down?

#4

Puzzler Answer:

RAY: The folks that Vinnie spotted? They were shivering, it was obviously cold in the car, and they were trying to wipe the condensing moisture off the windows.

TOM: Sure. So? Maybe they just started the car? It was cold out. You said, "It was a cold and blustery day"! I heard you.

RAY: Yes, but they *hadn't* just started the car. Vinnie knew that. He knew it because he didn't see any condensation coming out from the tailpipe.

TOM: Ah! Of course! When the engine's running, you burn hydrocarbons and you get what?

RAY: Carbon dioxide and water.

TOM: And that water comes out of the engine as steam, but on a cold day, as it travels through that long, cold tailpipe, it starts to condense back into water vapor, which is visible. And that's why you see a huge plume of vapor coming out of cars' tailpipes on cold mornings.

RAY: But once the exhaust system fully warms up, most of the water comes all the way out as steam, which is invisible. That's why the plume disappears on all but the coldest days.

TOM: So Vinnie knew that the engine was warmed up, yet the people inside the car were still shivering. That means he concluded...what? That either the heater was broken, or they were too stupid to turn the heat on. Which was it?

RAY: The heat obviously wasn't working, and while this could be due to a plugged heater core, Vinnie surmised that they were out of coolant. And if that were true, the engine would overheat before reaching the top of the next mountain.

TOM: Wow. Very good. I bet he charged them an arm and a leg to rescue them.

RAY: Of course! The letter said he was a "successful businessman"!

Winter in the Caprice.

Puzzler 5

The Cubed Car

RAY: This puzzler has to do with your old car, the Sleek Black Beauty.

TOM: My magnificent, black, 1965 AMC 990 Ambassador convertible? My favorite car of all time? What about it?

RAY: I had a dream that we took your car to the crusher.

TOM: Stop! I can't bear to listen to this. You're about to see a grown man cry.

RAY: Well, in the dream, the car was crushed into a 3- by 3- by 3-foot cube, and it went right onto the barge with all the other garbage, headed for its final resting place.

TOM: You're a cruel brother. No wonder Mom liked me better.

RAY: Anyway, as luck would have it, the cube falls in the water.

TOM: And sinks all the way to the bottom of Lake Gitchy Goomie.

RAY: Right. Assuming that water can't escape from the lake—the water level must either go up, go down, or stay the same. We'll assume, by the way, that this is a solid cube of rust. The question is this: When Tommy's former Sleek Black Beauty falls off the barge and into the lake, does the water level in the lake go down, go up, or does it stay the same?

#5

Puzzler Answer:

TOM: I didn't know the answer to this puzzler. I had to go try it out myself. You don't mind that I used your car, do you?

RAY: Not at all. The answer, by the way, is that the level of the lake goes down when the cube falls off the barge!

TOM: No kidding? That's not obvious to me.

RAY: Well, there isn't a whole lot that's obvious to you, now, is there? The reason the lake level goes down is that when the car falls to the bottom of the lake, it can only displace an amount of water that's equal to its volume.

TOM: What a peaceful, final resting place. All those fish swimming around—it's beautiful, tranquil.

RAY: When the 3,000-pound cube of crushed steel, headrests, and mice is in the barge, it displaces more water than it does when it's in the lake. Why? Because when the cube is in the barge, it's displacing its equivalent weight in water—which is the principle of buoyancy, and explains how destroyers, ducks, and barges float. A cubic foot of water weighs about 62.4 pounds*, so in this case, the barge holding the crushed Sleek Black Beauty must displace about 48 cubic feet of water [3,000 pounds of crushed steel divided by 62.4 equals about 48 cubic feet of water], in order to remain afloat.

$$62.4\overline{)3{,}000} = 48$$

When the Sleek Black Beauty cube sinks to the bottom, however, it can only displace an amount of water equal to its volume—and since it's a 3-foot cube, that's 27 cubic feet of water. So when Tommy's old jalopy sinks to the bottom, Lake Gitchy Goomie's water level goes down about 21 cubic feet.

$$\begin{array}{r} 48 \\ -27 \\ \hline =21 \end{array}$$

*According to a team of Boeing engineers who asked not to be publicly associated with our show.

#5

TOM: Hey. I know why this puzzler sounds familiar. Isn't this exactly what happened to Uncle Enzo after he squealed?

RAY: I don't think you want to talk about that. The statute of limitations hasn't expired yet.

TOM: By the way, you still owe me a '65 Ambassador convertible!

Ho Ho Ho this!

Eavesdropping at the Greasy Spoon

RAY: I was having lunch one Saturday morning last spring, at the counter of Sam's Luncheonette in our fair city. I was contemplating my tuna on light rye. Not having much else to do, I decided to engage in one of my favorite pastimes—eavesdropping.

TOM: You were eavesdropping on the guy next to you?

RAY: No, you moron, I was eavesdropping on a guy six blocks away. *Of course* I was eavesdropping on the guy next to me. Seated next to me was a young boy, and to his left was an older person who presumably was his father.

TOM: Or his mother. Remember, this was in Cambridge.

RAY: If it was his mom, she had one heck of a mustache. Anyway, they're scribbling some numbers on a napkin. I assume that the boy, who's about nine years old, is learning to add decimals. They write down the following numbers: 2.1, 4.2, 3.0, 3.2.

TOM: I've got 12.5.

RAY: Very good, that's exactly what I got. But they didn't get 12.5.

TOM: They didn't?

RAY: No. I know that they didn't because I was looking over the kid's shoulder. They got 13.2. I was about to say, "You morons," and I was going to tap the guy on the shoulder and tell him, "Gee, if you're going to teach the kid how to add decimals, you ought to at least do it right." Then they got up to leave.

TOM: Did they throw a cup of coffee in your face and say, "Mind your own business, buster"?

RAY: No. But as they got up to leave and put on their hats and jackets, I realized that their addition was correct.

TOM: It was?

RAY: It was. Why was 13.2 the right answer?

TOM: 'Cause you were doing it in Centigrade and they did it in Fahrenheit?

RAY: No.

#6

Puzzler Answer:

RAY: The clues were "spring," "Saturday," and "hats." As they left Sam's Luncheonette, I realized they were going to play baseball, and they were adding up innings pitched.

TOM: Ah ha! So how does that get to be 13.2?

RAY: Because innings are measured in thirds. Four-point-two is $4\frac{2}{3}$ of an inning pitched. Okay?

TOM: So 2.1 and 4.2 is 7.

RAY: Bingo.

TOM: This is in base three, is that right?

RAY: No, just the side to the right of the decimal is in base three. The other side is base ten.

TOM: That's interesting, the left side is base ten and the right side is base three.

RAY: I guess their gloves, bats, and spikes should have given it away sooner, huh?

TOM: Well, when the kid dropped his batting helmet on your sandwich, that might have tipped off a more perceptive person. But who can always pay that kind of close attention to things?

The Lady, the Tiger, and the King

RAY: Once upon a time, long, long ago, in a place far, far away, there was...what?

TOM: A kingdom?

RAY: Good. And in the kingdom there lived... what?

TOM: A king!

RAY: Very good. And the king had a beautiful daughter, who wanted to wed. The king, however, did not want her to leave his side, so he designed a series of tests that suitors would have to pass. There were tests of bravery, strength, and athletic prowess.

TOM: I'm sort of picturing the whole thing, a kind of Camelot scene. I can see this nice guy riding up on his horse, sidesaddle.

RAY: Actually, he was driving a VW bus. Anyway, once a suitor had passed all of the physical tests, he had to complete the final task, which no previous suitor had ever survived. He had to reach into a large box and draw out a slip of paper, which foretold his fate.

TOM: It couldn't have been a box. It must have been a big brass bowl—or solid gold.

RAY: Actually, it was a brown paper bag. The suitor would reach into the bag. Inside were two slips of paper. One piece of paper had the words, "The Tiger" on it and the other one said, "The Lady." If he should be so fortunate as to pick the piece of paper that said "The Lady" on it, he would marry the princess and be heir to the throne—once he figured out how to bump off the king. However, if he was unfortunate enough to pick the piece of paper that said, "The Tiger," he would be led outside led outside, to a caged area, and shortly thereafter would be passing through the digestive system of a large cat. As you might imagine, suitors came...and suitors went.

TOM: They were all unsuitable suitors?

RAY: Well, they all drew the piece of paper that said "The Tiger."

TOM: Talk about bad luck!

RAY: Well, it may not have been "bad luck." Picture this: A suitor comes along—tall, dark, and handsome. The princess takes a shine to this guy...

TOM: What's his name?

RAY: Prince Valiant. Prince Plymouth Valiant. She pulls him aside and says to him, "I think my father cheats. I think that inside the paper bag there are really two pieces of paper that both say, "The Tiger."

TOM: That cad!

RAY: Prince Plymouth says, "No problem. Let me worry about passing the pole-vaulting test and the blueberry pie-eating contest. Once I do that, I will win your hand." She asks, "How are you going to do it?" And he says, "Don't worry, I've got a plan." He's not going to use any sleight of hand, and he knows that he cannot expose the king as a cheat.

TOM: Of course not. That would be vulgar.

RAY: So when the moment comes, after he's passed all of the tests, Prince Plymouth reaches into the bag and he pulls out one of the two pieces of paper that is in there. He knows already what it says on it because he knows...what?

TOM: The king's a cheat!

RAY: Right. How does the prince pull it off?

#7

Puzzler Answer:

RAY: The suitor reads what he has chosen, jumps for joy, and says, "I *won!*"...and immediately swallows the paper.

TOM: What if the king had it on an 8$\frac{1}{2}$-by-11 sheet of paper?

RAY: Hey, you can do a lot when you know the tiger is waiting. So everyone in the court asks, "What did it say?" The prince replies, "It said, 'The Lady.' Look—as the king will show you—the remaining paper says, 'The Tiger.'"

TOM: Wow! What did the king have to say about this?

RAY: I think he must probably have muttered, "Gee...I guess you win."

TOM: Otherwise, he'd have had to divulge the fact that he was a sleazeball.

RAY: Well, the last I heard is that he was calling for the stomach pump!

Sister Mary Ellen brings Tom to his knees with a deft karate move, Boston Symphony Hall, June 30, 1994.

Puzzler 8

The Monty Hall
"Let's Make a Deal" Puzzler

RAY: Many years ago on television, there was a show called "Let's Make a Deal."

TOM: And people from the audience would yell out, "Take the chicken livers! Take the chicken livers!"

RAY: That's the one. The host was a fellow named Monty Hall, and his lovely assistant was Carol Merrill. The show consisted of people trying to win prizes and they would do so by picking one of three doors.

TOM: There was one good prize and two "zonks": crummy prizes, like a lifetime's supply of Preparation H or Eskimo Pies. Or both.

RAY: Monty would say, "Pick a door." And then you would pick a door. Now, let's say you picked Door Number One.

TOM: So your chances of winning the good prize are one out of three.

RAY: Right. So you pick Door Number One, and Monty now says, "Do you want to stick with that door or would you like to switch and take one of the other doors?" Now, everyone knows that if you switch, your chances of winning the big prize don't change.

TOM: It's still one in three. One in three is one in three.

RAY: But get this: Monty then says to you, "How about if I show you what's behind one of the doors that you didn't pick?"

TOM: But Monty knows which one is the winning door, and he's not going to show you the winner, right?

RAY: Right. He's going to show you a zonk. So he opens Door Number Two. It's the six boxes of Eskimo Pies.

TOM: Good thing I didn't get those. I'm lactose intolerant!

RAY: Then he asks you a final time, "Are you sure you don't want to switch?" And that is the question: *After* Monty shows you that zonk behind Door Number Two, should you switch?

#8

Puzzler Answer:

RAY: Let me preface this answer by saying that this question has generated more controversy than any of the other crummy puzzlers we've used over the last ten years.

TOM: When we first had this puzzler on our show, we had thousands of people who wrote in...all with the wrong answer—including some very learned mathematics professors from throughout this great land of ours—especially from M.I.T. and Harvard.

RAY: The short answer is "You should switch."

TOM: Get out!

RAY: Absolutely true! There are lots of different ways to explain why. The one that I think is the best explanation is this: When you picked Door Number One, what if Monty then came along and said to you, "How you would like to swap your choice of Door Number One for Doors Number Two *and* Number Three?" You'd do it, wouldn't you?

TOM: Sure! And that's basically what's he's saying. He's showing you what's behind Door Number Two, and then he's offering you Door Number Three. Who wouldn't change one door for two?

RAY: If you don't believe us, play this game against somebody for money.

TOM: Just make sure you send us 10 percent of the earnings.

The Fallout from the Monty Hall "Let's Make a Deal" Puzzler

A lot of times, a puzzler we present will stir up a minor controversy. Perhaps a few letters, some criticism. Sometimes, we even get a genuine stack of mail, explaining how, in no uncertain terms, we have our headlights squarely in our taillight sockets.

And then, there is the Monty Hall "Let's Make A Deal" Puzzler.

Never has a "Car Talk" puzzler caused such strife! Our answer sent thousands of Ivy League math professors scurrying to their word processors, eager to prove us wrong—and use the letter as a "publication" in the eyes of the tenure committee. Some even stopped by the garage to "explain" how wrong we were!

Being stubborn ignoramuses, however, we insisted we had the correct answer. We even got help from some unlikely quarters. Professor Steve Selvin wrote us, with the formal proof that vindicated us. Monty Hall even wrote in, proving to us that, just like Martin Gardner, he's still alive too.

In the end, we were vindicated. (That, in itself, came as quite a shock.) If you don't believe us, you can go to our Web site, the "Car Talk" section of cars.com. After we used the Monty Hall puzzler on the show, we actually had to build a demonstration game to prove our detractors wrong. We've now had over 30,000 people play our computer simulation, and we show the number who have won by switching…and the number who have won by *not* switching. There are twice as many winners among the switchers. Good, huh?

The Monty Hall puzzler is truly the zenith of all puzzlers. The standard by which all other puzzlers are measured. The pinnacle of our most lofty puzzler aspirations. We hope you enjoy it.

And if you disagree with our answer…tough luck!

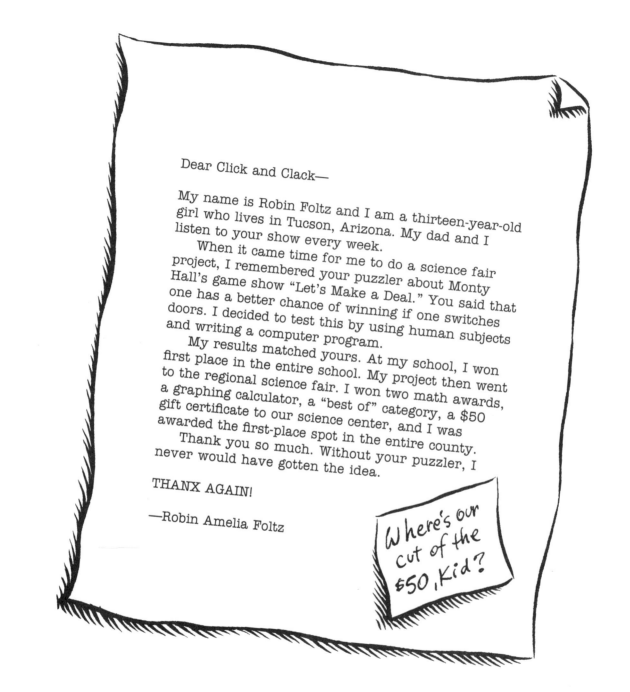

Dear Click and Clack—

My name is Robin Foltz and I am a thirteen-year-old girl who lives in Tucson, Arizona. My dad and I listen to your show every week.

When it came time for me to do a science fair project, I remembered your puzzler about Monty Hall's game show "Let's Make a Deal." You said that one has a better chance of winning if one switches doors. I decided to test this by using human subjects and writing a computer program.

My results matched yours. At my school, I won first place in the entire school. My project then went to the regional science fair. I won two math awards, a graphing calculator, a "best of" category, a $50 gift certificate to our science center, and I was awarded the first-place spot in the entire county.

Thank you so much. Without your puzzler, I never would have gotten the idea.

THANX AGAIN!

—Robin Amelia Foltz

Where's our cut of the $50, Kid?

Letter to the Editor of *The American Statistician* I, February 1975

A PROBLEM IN PROBABILITY

It is "Let's Make a Deal"—a famous TV show starring Monty Hall.

Monty Hall: One of the three boxes labeled A, B, and C contains the keys to the new 1975 Lincoln Continental. The other two are empty. If you choose the box containing the keys, you win the car.

Contestant: Gasp!

Monty Hall: Select one of the boxes.

Contestant: I'll take Box B.

Monty Hall: Now box A and box C are on the table and here is box B (contestant grips box B tightly). It is possible the car keys are in that box! I'll give you $100 for the box.

Contestant: No, thank you.

Monty Hall: How about $200?

Contestant: No!

Audience: No!

Monty Hall: Remember that the probability of your box containing the keys to the car is $\frac{1}{3}$ and the probability of your box being empty is $\frac{2}{3}$. I'll give you $500.

Audience: No!!

Contestant: No, I think I'll keep this box.

Monty Hall: I'll do you a favor and open one of the remaining boxes on the table (he opens box A). It's empty! (Audience: applause.) Now either box C or your box B contains the car keys. Since there are two boxes left, the probability of your box containing the keys is now $\frac{1}{2}$, I'll give you $1,000 cash for your box.

WAIT!!!!

Is Monty right? The contestant knows that at least one of the boxes on the table is empty. He now knows it was box A. Does this knowledge change his probability of having the box containing the keys from $\frac{1}{3}$ to $\frac{1}{2}$? One of the boxes on the table has to be empty. Has Monty done the contestant a favor by showing him which of the two boxes was empty? Is the probability of winning the car $\frac{1}{2}$ or $\frac{1}{3}$?

Contestant: I'll trade you my box B for the box C on the table.

Monty Hall: That's weird!

HINT: The contestant knows what he is doing!

Solution to "A Problem in Probability"

Certainly Monty Hall knows which box is the winner and, therefore, would not open the box containing the keys to the car. Consider all possible outcomes:

Keys are in box	Contestant chooses box	Monty Hall opens box	Contestant switches	Result
A	A	B or C	A for B or C	loses
A	B	C	B for A	wins
A	C	B	C for A	wins
B	A	C	A for B	wins
B	B	A or C	B for A or C	loses
B	C	A	C for B	wins
C	A	B	A for C	wins
C	B	A	B for C	wins
C	C	A or B	C for A or B	loses

Enumeration shows probability of winning is $\frac{6}{9} - \frac{2}{3}$. If the contestant does not switch boxes, then his probability of winning the car remains unchanged ($\frac{1}{3}$) after Monty Hall opens an additional box.

monty hall

May 12, 1975

Mr. Steve Selvin
Asst. Professor of Biostatistics
University of California, Berkeley
Earl Warren Hall
Berkeley, California 94720

Dear Steve:

Thank you for sending me the problem from "The American Statistician."

Although I am not a student of statistics problems, I do know that these figures can always be used to one's advantage, if I wished to manipulate same. The big hole in your argument of problems is that once the first box is seen to be empty, the contestant cannot exchange his box. So the problems still remain the same, don't they ... one out of three. Oh, and incidentally, after one is seen to be empty, his chances are no longer 50/50 but remain what they were in the first place, one out of three. It just seems to the contestant that one box having been eliminated, he stands a better chance. Not so. It was always two to one against him. And if you ever get on my show, the rules hold fast for you -- no trading boxes after the selection.

Next time let's play on my home grounds. I graduated in chemistry and zoology. You want to know your chances of surviving with our polluted air and water?

Sincerely,

monty

Letter to the Editor of *The American Statistician* II, August 1975

ON THE MONTY HALL PROBLEM

I have received a number of letters commenting on my "Letter to the Editor" in *The American Statistician* of February, 1975, entitled "A Problem in Probability." Several correspondents claim my answer is incorrect. The basis to my solution is that Monty Hall knows which box contains the keys and when he can open either of two boxes without exposing the keys, he chooses between them at random. An alternative solution to enumberating the mutually exclusive and equally likely outcomes is as follows:

A = event that keys are contained in box B
B = event that contestant chooses box B
C = event that Monty Hall opens box A

Then:
P (keys in box B | Contestant chooses B and Monty Hall opens A)

$$= P(A \text{ keys in box B } BC) = P(ABC)/P(BC)$$
$$= P(C \mid AB)P(AB)/P(C \mid B)P(B)$$
$$= P(C \mid AB)P(B \mid A)/P(A)/P(C \mid B)P(B)$$
$$= (1/2)\,(1/3)\,(1/3)\,(1/2)\,(1/3)$$

If the contestant B trades his box B for the unopened box on the table, his probability of winning the car is $2/3$.

D.L. Ferguson presented a generalization of this probelm for the case of n boxes, in which Monty Hall opens p boxes. In this situation, the probability the contestant wins when he switches boxes is:

$$[(n - 1)[n(n - p - 1)].$$

Benjamin King pointed out the critical assumptions about Monty Hall's behavior that are necessary to solve the problem, and emphasized that "the prior distribution is not the only part of the probabilistic side of a decision problem that is subjective."

Monty Hall wrote and expressed that he was not "a student of statistics problems" but "the big hole in your argument is that once the first box is seen to be empty, the contestant cannot exchange his box." He continues to say, "Oh, and incidentally, after one [box] is seen to be empty, his chances are no longer 50/50 but remain what they were in the first place, one out of three. It just seems to the contestant that one box having been eliminated, he stands a better chance. Not so." I could not have said it better myself.

For Dessert Only?

RAY: When I was but a boy in the 1950s, I remember getting into a Rambler of one kind or another.

TOM: Ah, the '50s. I remember them well.

RAY: Of course you remember them well. You've never left the '50s. Anyway, on the right side of the dash were the heater controls. There were controls for heat, for

defrost, and for temperature. And then there was a lever that said: "For Desert Only."

TOM: You were just a little, wee lad. Are you sure it didn't say, "For Dessert Only"? Maybe it dispensed a piece of pound cake?

RAY: No. The idea was, if you were driving in the desert, you would engage this device, whatever it was. You would push this lever, and it would somehow make the vehicle run better, or do something that would assist you in getting across the desert without trouble. The question is: What on earth was this thing?

Puzzler Answer:

RAY: This lever would activate the heater, but it would divert the heat outside the car.

TOM: Wait a minute, so you're adding heat to the desert? Isn't that kind of redundant?

RAY: Precisely. And by doing so, you were helping to cool the engine. You see, the heater core acts just like another little section of radiator, removing heat from the engine. Normally, the heat you pull off the engine is used to warm up the passenger compartment.

TOM: But by diverting the heat outside, this little knob kept the passengers from dying of heatstroke. That was brilliant of them!

RAY: It took some experimenting, and I think a number of AMC engineers expired in the process. There's a memorial to them in the Mojave, I believe.

TOM: Boy, those guys at AMC were on the cutting edge of technology, weren't they?

RAY: No.

Ray, involved in yet another industrial accident at the garage.

The Boy, the Bus, and the Fishing Rod

RAY: Here's a puzzler that revolves around numbers. A young boy is standing—

TOM: Numbers? How old is he?

RAY: He's eleven.

TOM: All right, an eleven-year-old boy.

RAY: An eleven-year-old boy is standing at the bus stop waiting for the bus.

TOM: What number bus?

RAY: The number twelve bus.

TOM: Okay.

RAY: And it's about 12:30 in the afternoon. And he's standing there with the new fishing rod he just bought.

TOM: How long is the fishing rod?

RAY: Five feet. The bus stops, and the boy attempts to enter the bus, and the bus driver stops the boy as he puts that first foot in the door and says to him, "Nah, you can't get on." And the kid asks why.

TOM: Wait—how many times did the kid ask why?

RAY: Just one time. The bus driver says there's a city ordinance—

TOM: What number?

RAY: Number 113, which prohibits anyone from carrying packages on the bus longer than four feet. So the kid says, "How am I supposed to get home?" The bus driver says, "That's your problem, kid. That fishing rod is about five feet long and I'm booting you out."

TOM: Boots him right out of the bus, huh?

RAY: He kicks him off, and the kid stands there bewildered. He decides he'll have to go back into the store and return the fishing rod. So he goes back to the store and they say, "No returns after fifteen minutes." So he's stuck with the fishing rod and no way to get home. He can't take a cab, since he doesn't have enough money. He has to take the bus and he's got this fishing rod that's five feet long.

He walks back into the store again, realizing he can't return it, and five minutes later he's on the bus with the fishing rod—without altering it, breaking it, sawing it in half, or collapsing it. He does nothing to alter the fishing rod. How does he do it?

#10

Puzzler Answer:

He goes back to the store where he bought the fishing rod and gets a box that's four feet by three feet, and the diagonal is five feet.

Plural Car Names

RAY: This puzzler came to us from a listener in some charming little place called King of Prussia, Pennsylvania.

TOM: That is a charming little place. With a charming little name.

RAY: Yes, it is a charming... Well, to be perfectly honest, isn't it kind of a strange name?

TOM: Downright bizarre! What the heck kind of name is that, anyway?

RAY: Well, speaking of names, here's the puzzler. Automobile model names are often nouns. For example, Mustang or Dart or Vista. Now, you wouldn't expect a manufacturer to use a plural noun. For example, you don't often hear of a car being called a Rivieras or an Accords?

TOM: No, you certainly don't.

RAY: But the practice is not completely unknown. Can you identify an automobile model the name of which is plural? We can think of two of them. If you can think of more than two, you can write your own puzzler book! And we're not counting numerals, letters like STS, the letter "S" as a trim level designation, or words whose plurals are the same as their singulars—like "sheep."

TOM: Right. We're looking for honest-to-goodness plural nouns slapped onto the trunk lids of cars.

11

Puzzler Answer

TOM: The answer must be Latin.

RAY: Good! You're absolutely right.

TOM: And it has to end in *ae*.

RAY: Wrong. The word actually ends in *a*. You have the wrong declension.

TOM: Wrong declension? My sixteen-year-old son was in declension the other day after school.

RAY: The answer is Maxima, the plural of *maximum*.

TOM: Maxima. Now, that's good!

RAY: And by the way, for you Latin nerds out there, Maxima is a second declension neuter adjective, which can also be used as a noun. Another plural name is Integra, which is the second declension plural of *integer*. Someone else suggested the Mazda Millenia, but that's wrong.

TOM: What's wrong about it? Sounds good to me—it's the plural of *millennium*.

RAY: It would be, but the boneheads at Mazda went and misspelled it. The plural of *millennium* would have two "n"s. So if Mazda changes the name of the car to *Millennia*, we'll include it in the next edition of this book.

Pills in the Pharmacy I

RAY: Imagine this scene...

TOM: Should I close my eyes?

RAY: You mean they were open? Our setting is a pharmacy. Behind the desk is a grizzled old pharmacist, and he's got a young assistant named George Bailey. The pharmacy has just received a shipment of pills—like, say, ten huge bottles of pills. And young George dutifully puts the jars of pills on the shelf. The next day, the older pharmacist says, "There's something wrong. One of the bottles we got has faulty pills. The pills in that one bottle are all 1 gram too heavy, and need to be sent back."

TOM: And am I to presume that he knows how much a real, non-counterfeit pill weighs?

RAY: Sure. He knows that a regular pill is supposed to weigh 5 grams and these faulty pills each weigh 6 grams. You can't tell by looking at them, so someone is faced with the prospect of having to go through the trouble of weighing a pill from each bottle, to find the bad jar.

TOM: What kind of medicine was this, anyway?

RAY: Extra-strength Rogaine. So the grizzled, mean, old pharmacist assigns this task to sweet little George. But George is about to go out on a date, and he doesn't want to take the time to weigh a pill from each bottle. George comes up with a way to determine which bottle is faulty—using the scale only one time.

TOM: Wow. One weighing?

RAY: Right. How does he do it?

Tom and Ray doing the show from a moving vehicle during the "witness protection years."

#12

Puzzler Answer:

RAY: Here's what George did: First, he numbered the jars from one to ten. Then he took one pill from the first bottle, two pills from the second bottle, three pills from the third, four pills from the fourth, and so on, and he ended up with fifty-five pills.

TOM: So, you mean that heap of pills should weigh 55 grams?

RAY: No, you moron. It should weigh fifty-five times 5 grams each, or 275 grams.

TOM: And what if it weighed 276?

RAY: Then you have one overweight pill and you'd know it came from what?

TOM: Bottle number one!

RAY: And if it weighed 278, you'd know you have three overweight pills and they came from where? Bottle number three. And so on and so forth. And because George is so clever, he finished the job in two minutes flat, and picks up his date on time.

TOM: Was she impressed?

RAY: No, he was driving a Dodge Dart.

Pills in the Pharmacy II: The Question Gets Harder

TOM: If you liked the last puzzler, you'll love this one.

RAY: It's exactly the same puzzler—with a little twist. We're back at the drugstore, with George Bailey and the grizzled old pharmacist. The shipment of pills has arrived.

TOM: Why this interest in pills lately? Have you been sick?

RAY: I've been getting queasy a lot. But only when I look in the mirror. This time around, there are six big bottles of pills.

TOM: Six bottles. Okay.

RAY: The catch is, there may be more than one bottle with defective, heavy pills that weigh 6 grams instead of 5. In fact, for all we know, all of the bottles might be defective!

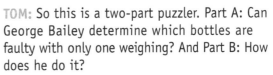

TOM: So this is a two-part puzzler. Part A: Can George Bailey determine which bottles are faulty with only one weighing? And Part B: How does he do it?

Puzzler Answer:

RAY: Our kid George is no slouch. He numbers the jars again. Then he takes one pill from the first bottle, two pills from the second, four from the next, eight from the next—

TOM: I love it already!

RAY: Sixteen from the next.

TOM: Let me guess. A geometric progression. Thirty-two from the last bottle?

RAY: Right, Tommy. So George weighs this entire pile of sixty-three pills. Then he multiplies sixty-three by five—

TOM: Which is how many grams the pills are supposed to weigh. I come up with 315 grams.

RAY: Right. And then, by subtracting 315 from the actual weight of the pile of pills, he can figure out which jar—or jars—have the heavy pills.

TOM: How, pray tell? Let's say the pile weighs 27 grams too much. How does he know which jars the overweight pills came from?

RAY: Well, there is only one way to get 27.

TOM: Oh. Like, the first bottle (one pill), plus the second bottle (two pills), plus the fourth bottle (eight pills), plus the fifth bottle (sixteen pills)?

RAY: Very good, Tommy! And no matter how much the weight is over, there's only one combination of bottles that will get you to that total. Why?

TOM: Because, as any nerd worth his pocket protector knows, you can express every integer as a sum of powers of two! That's the way your computer does it.

RAY: Pretty good, huh?

#13

A Haircut in Horse Town

RAY: Imagine this scene: A fellow is driving across the desert in Nevada, when all of a sudden he finds himself in urgent need of a haircut.

TOM: I didn't know you could find yourself in urgent need of a haircut.... What, he's just driving along, when suddenly he realizes, "Geez, I really need a haircut?"

RAY: Yes. Something like that. Actually, he said, "I need to *take* a haircut."

TOM: Right! "I gotta take a wicked haircut. I'll never make it to the next exit!"

RAY: Exactly. So he finds himself in desperate need of a haircut, and he takes the next exit: Exit 411, a little one-horse town named One

Horse, Nevada. And, as luck would have it, in One Horse, Nevada, there are two barbershops, so he has to decide which one to go to for a haircut. Our traveler goes to barbershop number one, and he looks in the window. There are no customers in that barbershop.

The barbershop is kind of messy, and even the barber—who is the only one in the place—is kind of messy, too. He's unshaven and has a lousy shirt on. There's hair on the floor, and even *his* haircut is lousy. So this fellow says to himself, "Maybe I should check out the other barbershop in One Horse." He moseys along, which is what you would do in One Horse, Nevada, if you were there.

He arrives at barbershop number two, and he looks in the window. It looks terrific. It's nice, and neat and clean. The mirrors are clean and shiny. Even the barber himself looks neat and well-groomed, with a great haircut.

TOM: Is he wearing one of those white jackets?

RAY: Of course—with the comb and the scissors in the pocket.

TOM: His name wasn't Mr. Gigi?

RAY: No. I think it was Bruno. As a matter of fact, the other guy's name was Bruno, too. So there it is. Barbershop number one: a pig sty and crummy-looking barber with a lousy haircut. Barbershop number two: neat place, well-groomed barber, nice white shop coat, comb in the pocket, and a great haircut. This is a two-part question.

Part A: Which barbershop does he choose?
Part II: How come he chooses the messy one?

#14

Puzzler Answer:

RAY: The answer is very simple. Tom didn't get it, but like I said, the answer is very simple. In One Horse, Nevada, there are only two barbershops, and it's perfectly logical that one barber must get his hair cut—

TOM: From the other barber! Like if there were two dentists. Hey, we could use this puzzler again with dentists. We can use it every week!

RAY: Two mechanics!

TOM: Two tailors!

RAY: Our traveler has to go to the barber with the lousy haircut, because he's the guy who cut the neat-looking barber's hair.

TOM: He got that haircut from the sloppy guy! Of course! Who else would he get it from?

RAY: The guy with the neat-looking shop is the lousy barber. Why is his shop so neat? He has no customers.

TOM: Neat, huh?

Tom and Ray doing the show from the winter palace at Vladivostok, January, 1941.

A Haircut in Horse Town:
The Legacy of "Car Talk"?

Longtime listeners of "Car Talk" (all six of you) will recognize that this is the puzzler that catapulted the phrase "taking a haircut" into the heart of the American lexicon. William Safire, please take note.

It was one of those times during the show when Tom and Ray momentarily lost their composure. The idea of "taking a wicked haircut" just sent them on a tear-streaming laugh that continued through the next several shows.

And thus, "taking a haircut" became equated with "using the porcelain facilities."

To our surprise (and to our mother's consternation), "taking a haircut" started to break out into daily conversation. Ray knew the phrase had made its way into modern usage when he overheard Martha Stewart telling her guests that she had to "run out to take a haircut" at The Four Seasons restaurant in New York City. Tommy swears that when the guys performed at the White House a few years back, Vice President Gore whispered to the boss that he'd be right back after "a quick haircut."

One thing we do know: If "taking a haircut" is going to become commonplace, we're going to need your help! Please use it often. And in doing so, you'll be contributing to the lasting legacy of "Car Talk." We thank you.

Motel Four and the Missing Dollar

RAY: Ken Rogers, Bugsy Lawlor, and our producer Dougie Berman go on a little junket. They decide to stay at a Motel Four.

TOM: Being the cheapskates they are, they all decide to share one room. They ask for the cheapest room available, and for 30 bucks, they get the laundry room. So they each give the desk clerk a $10 bill.

RAY: After they check in, however, the desk clerk realizes that he accidentally overcharged them. It turns out that there's a special on the laundry room, and it's only 25 bucks a night. So he calls for the chambermaid, Lenny.

TOM: And he tells Lenny, "You know those three nerds who checked into Room 18? Here's 5 bucks. Go give it to them."

RAY: Lenny's smart, however, and he realizes that he's dealing with three public radio types who won't be able to split $5 amongst the three of them. He says to himself, "Hmmm, how am I going to do this?" Here's what he decides to do: He shoves $2 in his pocket, and then shuffles up to Ken, Bugsy, and Dougie. He says, "Hey, look guys, they made a mistake. The room

Our Esteemed Producer, Doug Berman, spends many hours a day on his computer.

was only 27 bucks." Lenny gives them each a dollar and says, "You're all set." And they say, "Oh, great! Now we can buy dinner." Lenny walks away.

TOM: So here's the question: If each guy paid 10 bucks and got a dollar back, that's 9 bucks each. Nine times 3 is 27. Lenny pockets $2. That's $29. Where's the other buck?

final art

#15

Puzzler Answer:

RAY: It's a trick question. We were trying to dazzle you with fancy footwork. There is no missing dollar.

TOM: Right. The way we stated the puzzler would have you believe they spent $27 on the room and another 2 bucks on Lenny. But that wasn't the case. The hotel got $25 dollars for the room. Lenny pocketed $2, and gave them $3 back. That adds up to $30!

So they each spent $9 total: $8.33 each for the room—and 67 cents each for Lenny.

RAY: They're not so smart, are they?

TOM: No, they're not. But we've known that for quite some time now, haven't we?

RAY: By the way, we can't claim authorship to this puzzler. It has ancient roots, going back to, like, the three wise men.

TOM: Right. In that version, this all took place at the Bethlehem Hyatt.

Tom and Ray waving to the Pope, from their balcony in Harvard Square.

Tommy's Wives, Part One

RAY: Here's the new puzzler—and I'm going to make it about you, Tommy. Back in the old days—when you used to work—you used to have your wife drive you to the train station. Then, if I remember correctly, you'd take the train and go to work. After say, three or four hours of sleeping at your desk, you'd get back on the train and come home.

TOM: After lunch, you mean?

RAY: Right, after lunch. You'd get to the train station, and like she did every day, your wife would meet you there at the appointed hour and drive you to your Barcalounger. Well, one day you decided to leave work an hour early.

TOM: Like, before lunch.

RAY: Right. Needless to say, you got to the hometown train station an hour early. It was a nice day, and rather than call your wife, you decided to hoof it. So you started walking in the opposite direction she'd be driving. Lo and behold, you saw your wife coming up the road and she saw you by the side of road.

TOM: What was I doing by the side of the road?

RAY: "Taking a haircut," so to speak. You got in the car and you drove home, arriving twenty minutes earlier than usual. Now don't forget, she left home at the usual time.

TOM: Of course she did, because she didn't know I was going to leave work an hour early.

RAY: You got home twenty minutes earlier than you would have gotten home normally. So how long were you walking before you met your wife? Notice, there's no mention of how long she was driving, how fast Tommy walked, what number train he took, or what any of the distances were.

#16

Puzzler Answer:

TOM: I got it. I was walking for forty minutes.

RAY: So close.

TOM: Forty-five?

RAY: Closer.

TOM: Forty-six?

RAY: You're just guessing, aren't you? Fifty is the answer, and here's why: If you arrived home twenty minutes earlier than usual, by walking you saved ten minutes of your wife's travel time to the station and ten minutes of her travel time from the station. Therefore, you were walking for fifty minutes when she picked you up.

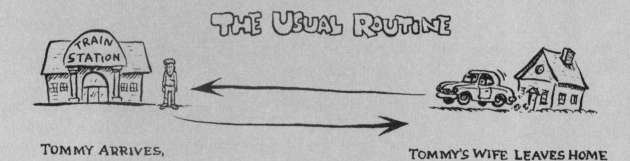

THE USUAL ROUTINE

TOMMY ARRIVES,
5:00 P.M.

TOMMY'S WIFE LEAVES HOME
AT 4:45, GETS BACK AT 5:15

TOM: You have to put all of the pieces together to get this one. I left an hour earlier, but my wife left at the same time, and all this saves twenty minutes off the total trip. So it's as if I moved the station ten minutes closer, by car. By the way, which wife was this?

RAY: Number one, I believe.

BUT TODAY...

BUT TODAY, TOMMY ARRIVES AT 4:00 P.M. AND WALKS FOR 50 MINUTES

STILL LEAVES AT 4:45, RETURNS 20 MINUTES EARLIER THAN USUAL-4:55

 The Case of the Bad Shocks

RAY: The other day, a woman we'll call Donna came into the shop. Donna said, "I went to one of those Speedy Gonzales muffler-brake-alignment-tune-up-falafel-liposuction-pedicure-burrito places."

TOM: The kind of place that you always bad-mouth and we get all the nasty mail from?

RAY: That's the place. She continued, "The guy told me, 'I'll show you that you need new shocks,' and he bounced up and down on my rear bumper." Donna's car went *boinga boinga boinga boinga boinga*. It kept going up and down, up and down, up and down. Finally she said, "Alright, already, put them in." So the mechanic put the shocks in, and she drove away. And, as luck would have it, they closed up shop the minute she left.

TOM: Some of those places are designed so that, as you back out, the building disappears!

RAY: Donna was very disappointed, because the ride was terrible—much worse than it had been with the old, lousy shocks in there. It felt like she was driving over cobblestone streets. So she went back the next morning and said, "There's something wrong with these shocks. They're obviously defective." So the mechanic proceeded to check them out and pronounced the shocks to be perfect. He did the bounce test. The car went *boinga* once and came to a complete stop, just as it should have. He said again, "There's nothing wrong with these shocks," and he threw her out of the garage. In desperation, she came to us.

TOM: She must have been at the end of her rope.

RAY: End of her rope? She was halfway done with the knot and was looking for a tree! She said, "Boys, what's wrong with my car? What did those bozos do to it?" We checked it out, and found that the muffler shop had done nothing wrong. Why was her ride so bad?

#17

Puzzler Answer:

RAY: The mechanic, in fact, did not do anything wrong. However, he did overlook one thing. She had way too much air in her tires. Like maybe fifty pounds of pressure in each tire. She never noticed this with the other shocks because they were so bad that when she hit bumps, the whole car went up and down, up and down, up and down.

TOM: *Boinga boinga boinga!*

RAY: And that's not very safe, because the purpose of the shocks is to keep the car from bouncing. That way, the wheels stay firmly on the ground. That's an important safety feature, especially when you want to do things like turn and stop.

TOM: But, the soft, worn-out shocks did mask the fact that she had too much air in her tires, and gave her a very soft ride—just like the *QE2*.

RAY: So we let that evil air out of the tires—

TOM: And that was it. How much did you charge her?

RAY: Fifteen hundred dollars. I had a boat payment coming up.

Ray makes freshly squeezed orange juice for the nice boys at the garage.

The Black Pearls Puzzler

RAY: Valentine's Day was recently upon us, and once again I was confronted with the dilemma of what to get my wife. This time I thought I'd do something unique. For years now, she's been asking for a string of black pearls. Black pearls are very rare—the only place they're found is in the waters off of the Seychelles—you know, those islands in the Indian ocean where they just did the latest edition of the *Sports Illustrated* swimsuit issue. These black pearls are brought up from the depths by divers who go down 200 feet with knives clenched in their teeth. If there's one of these pearls down there, they of course bring it to the surface. And if not, they eat the oysters.

Yes, that is Dr. Joyce Brothers. . . and she wasn't able to help at all.

TOM: Of course, the divers are always getting the bends. So they need to keep getting new divers...

RAY: Anyway, my wife asked for these pearls, and I said, "Geez, honey, these are a lot of money." So I proposed a little game. What I do is this: I get fifty of these black pearls and I put 'em in a cigar box. Then I get fifty cheap, faux white pearls and put them in a different cigar box. You following me? So I have box A with fifty black pearls.

TOM: And box number two, with fifty cheap white pearls.

RAY: Right. I tell my darling wife, "You can divide the pearls up any way you want between the two boxes—all the black ones in one box, all the whites in another, or any other imaginable combination. Then," I tell her, "I'm going to blindfold you, and I'm going to shuffle the boxes a few times. Then you tap one of the boxes with your finger and pick a pearl from inside that box. Whichever kind of pearl you pick, that's what you get for Valentine's Day." Got it? Now since there are fifty of each kind of pearl, what do you think her chances are?

TOM: Fifty-fifty, right?

RAY: Perhaps. That's my question. Is there any way she can mix up these pearls in the two boxes to improve her chances beyond fifty-fifty?

#18

Puzzler Answer:

RAY: You wouldn't think there would be a way for her to improve her odds, but there is.

TOM: I'm waiting! I'm ready! Lay it on me!

RAY: Remember now, she can do anything she wants with the pearls.

TOM: Got it. Any permutation.

RAY: And she has to use all the pearls.

TOM: Got it!

RAY: And she has to put them in these two boxes.

TOM: Alright, already. So what's the answer?

RAY: She can move all the pearls to one of the boxes—except for one black one.

TOM: Whoa! And she leaves that one black pearl in box number two?

RAY: You know, you're not so dumb after all. So she will certainly get a black pearl and if she picks box number two, and her chances are still pretty close to fifty-fifty in box number one, right?

TOM: Right! So her overall chances of getting a black pearl are close to 75 percent. I'm going to figure out the exact odds tonight when I have nothing else to do.

RAY: You always have nothing else to do!

The Six Wooden Matches

RAY: Imagine that you have six wooden matchsticks.

TOM: Got it.

RAY: Of length "M."

TOM: Okay.

RAY: Here's the puzzler: With these six matchsticks, make four identical triangles, all of which have a side equal to length M.

TOM: You can do that?

RAY: I can. Whether you can is another question altogether.

TOM: In other words, make four identical, equilateral triangles with six matchsticks.

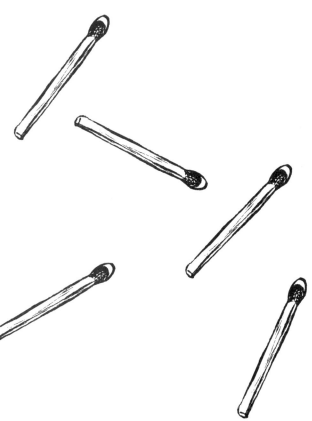

#19

Puzzler Answer:

TOM: This was one of the few puzzlers that I was able to solve in a relatively short amount of time. Like a week.

RAY: To figure this out, you have to use three dimensions.

TOM: That's tough for a guy like me. I'm still working in one dimension.

RAY: Here's what you do. You take three of the matchsticks, and you make a triangular base.

Then take the other three matchsticks and prop them up so they touch at the middle some place. And you will have, in fact, four triangles made out of six matchsticks.

TOM: You're very clever, do you know that? Did you figure that out all by yourself?

RAY: No, my eight-year-old son got it, and I held him upside down until he gave me the answer.

Ray and NPR's Scott Simon enjoy a light moment after beating Tom senseless with baseball bats.

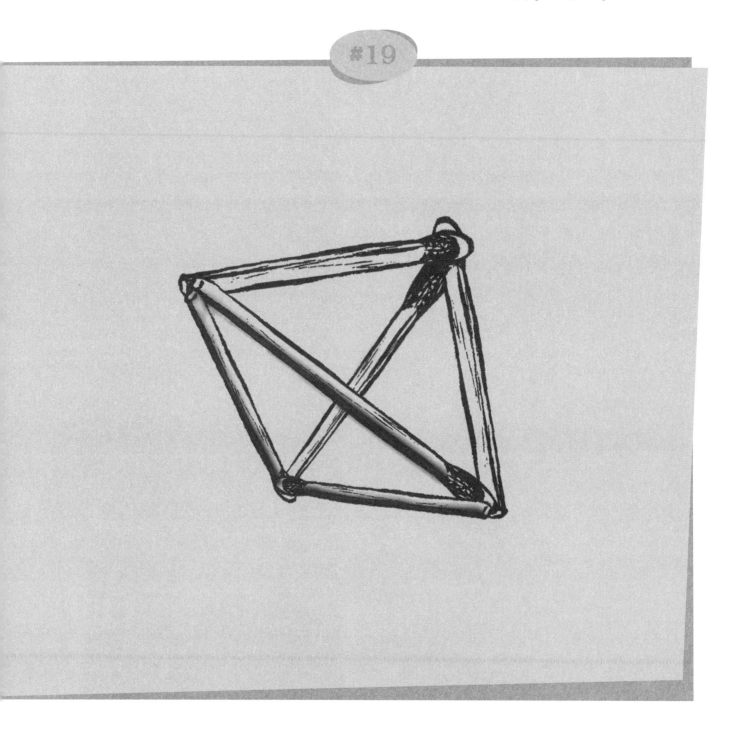

Puzzler 20

How High Can You Count Without Taking off Your Shoes?

RAY: The statement of this puzzle is extremely simple. It is, first of all, a nonautomotive puzzle.

TOM: Is it also nonintellectual?

RAY: We'll let our listeners be the judge of that. The beauty of this puzzler is its brevity.

TOM: It's short and to the point?

RAY: Yes, it's wonderfully short and succinct.

TOM: I'm sure you'll screw that up. You're well on the road to doing that already.

RAY: No, really, it is a truly elegant puzzler.

TOM: It's elegant in its brevity?

RAY: In its simplicity. In all its glorious brevity. Here it is, in a nutshell.

TOM: Is that a walnut shell?

RAY: Shut up! Here's the puzzler. Most of us have ten fingers—five on each hand. And we all know how to count to ten on those fingers.

TOM: Right. And then I have to take my shoes off when I get to eleven.

RAY: However, there is a way you can count to a much higher number with just those ten fingers. The question is: How high a number can you count to, without any ambiguity or confusion?

TOM: You mean, for example, you can't take your index finger and raise it a quarter of the way up to indicate one—and halfway up to indicate two.

RAY: No. That would be ambiguous and confusing and would obfuscate the truly elegant nature of this puzzler.

TOM: This brief puzzler.

RAY: Well, it was going to be brief. Here's one hint. This requires a certain amount of dexterity, one might say. Mr. Spock might find this easier to do than most of us mere humans.

#20

Puzzler Answer:

RAY: Ready?

TOM: I'm ready, man!

RAY: Okay. Hold your hands up—two fists—with no fingers sticking out.

That's the number zero. Now raise the pinky on your right hand. That's the number 1. Lower that and raise your ring finger on your right hand. That's the number 2. The next number is the number 3—that's your pinky and your ring finger.

TOM: Oh, that's what you've been signaling to me all these years! Four! Wait a minute...4 what?

RAY: What we're doing, is counting in base two. How high can you count? Well, my pinky finger is 2 to the zero power (equals 1), my ring finger is 2 to the first (equals 2), my middle finger is 2 to the second (equals 4), and so on....all the way up to 2 to the ninth. If I had eleven fingers,

I could count to the number 1,024. But I don't have eleven fingers, I have ten fingers, and therefore I can count one less than that: 1,023. In other words, it's 512, plus 256, plus 128, plus 64, plus 32, plus 16, plus 8, plus 4, plus 2, plus 1.

TOM: Pretty good. And if you used all your toes, too?

RAY: That's 1,048,575. By the way, we have to thank our friend Vito P. Maglione, who gave us this puzzler.

TOM: Thanks, Vito! See you at your parole party. When is that, anyway?

RAY: 2039, I think.

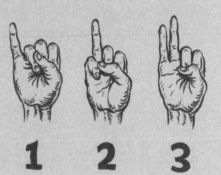

1   2   3

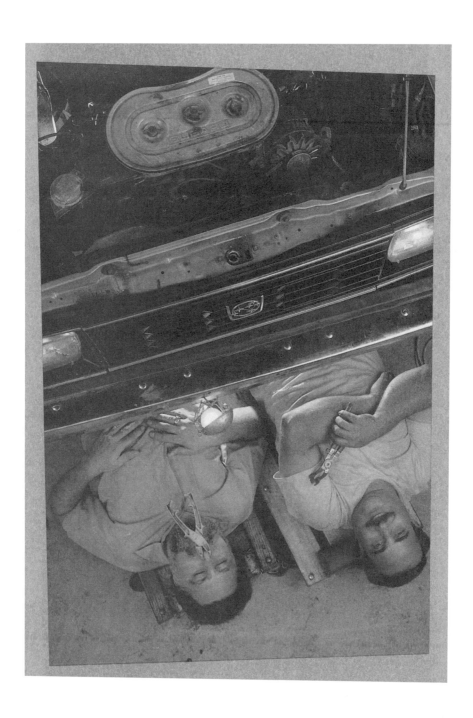

Puzzler 21

Our Fair City

RAY: A gentleman comes up to a bank teller in Boston and presents the following story. He says, "Hello there, young man, I'm visiting your fair city. "

TOM: "Our Fair City "? He really said it like that? Did this take place in the 1800s?

RAY: Actually, it was last week.

TOM: I like it! "Our Fair City "! I'm going to use that!

RAY: The fellow goes on to say, "I am an English professor from Northwestern University visiting your fair city with my wife and my two daughters, and I find myself in a most awkward situation. I have absolutely no money, and I'd be most grateful if you would cash a check for me. "

TOM: Polite guy, isn't he?

RAY: The teller says, "I don't see why that should be a problem." To which the visitor replies, "Unfortunately, all I have is a check. I don't have any identification because my wife and my oldest daughter took my wallet with all my credit cards and money, and they went off shopping."

TOM: Him, too, huh? That's always happening to me!

RAY: He continues, "All I have is this check with my name on it. It's a check from home. I assure you it's good. I wonder if you would be kind enough to cash it for $200." The teller looks at the professor, who is very well dressed, seemingly very articulate, and says, "I'll be right back."

TOM: ...I have to go talk to my sales manager. We may have a deal here!

RAY: A minute later, the teller comes back with Vinnie the Bouncer, and they throw the bum out.

TOM: They didn't!

RAY: They did! They refused to cash his check, and asked him to kindly leave the premises. How did they know he was a fraud?

21

Puzzler Answer:

RAY: The bank teller knew that the guy was a fraud because he made a mistake that a real English professor would never have made. He said he had two daughters. Then he referred to "My wife and my *oldest* daughter."

TOM: That's right. He should have said, "My *older* daughter."

RAY: You need to have three children to have an *oldest* child. A real English professor from Northwestern would have known that.

TOM: Of course, if he was from MIT, it would've been a different story.

RAY: Why? Does their grammar stink?

TOM: No—they don't have any English professors! That's why.

Restoring NPR's Luster via Highfalutin Language

"Hello there, young man, I'm an English professor from Northwestern University, and I'm visiting your fair city." So starts the "Our Fair City" puzzler. When Ray first delivered those lines many moons ago, Tom was struck with an uncontrollable fit of laughter. "'Our Fair City'???" he asked, with tears running down his face from laughing so hard. "Did he really say that?" "I don't know," said Ray, "it's just a puzzler!"

Such highfalutin language had rarely, if ever, found its way onto "Car Talk." Which may be why Tommy latched onto it...and hasn't let go since.

From then on, every time the address is given on the show, Tommy waits for Ray to get to "Cambridge," and then interjects, "Our Fair City!" By using such language, Tommy believes he is somehow restoring some of the luster "Car Talk" has taken off of NPR. He believes he's adding erudition, refinement, and enlightenment. "He's just interrupting me," says Ray.

In any case, Cambridge, Massachusetts, is now, and will be forever more, "Our Fair City." So if you ever find yourself visiting Our Fair City, be sure to stop by and give Tommy a dope slap for starting this silliness, will you?

A Tale of Two Brothers

TOM: There are two brothers who are well versed...

RAY: Are they poets?

TOM: No. They're well versed—in automotive technology. For better or for verse. And one of them is a real jamoke, who drives around in a 1974 Chevy.

RAY: Gee, who could that be? Wait a minute. Is there a family of raccoons living in the backseat?

TOM: There are raccoons...and huskies. They get along. Did you know that?

RAY: Yeah, when the wildebeests keep them apart. Does this guy have a petting zoo in the backseat?

TOM: So one brother—we'll call him brother A—drives around in a '74 Chevy. The other brother is sort of a "motorhead," so to speak. We'll call him brother two. In fact, he happens to drive race cars. He drives every year in the Indianapolis—or is it Minneapolis?—500.

RAY: Right, right. Mindianapolis. He drives in the Mindianapolis 500.

TOM: One day, brother A with the '74 Chevy challenges brother two to a race around the Mindianapolis Speedway, but instead of a 500-mile race, he challenges him to a 50-mile race.

RAY: Because he knows his car won't make it for 500 miles?

TOM: Bingo. He figures his car will make it 50 miles, tops. Brother A has only two stipulations. One, neither brother can make any alterations to his vehicle.

RAY: Do you mean to say that the '74 Chevy stays exactly how it always has been, with the raccoons in the back?

TOM: Correct. The huskies are on the left side, the raccoons are on the right side. And the race car is in the hangar, all ready to go. The second stipulation is that brother A gets to choose when they race. So brother two says, "You're on, piston-puss!" A few weeks go by, and one day the phone rings at brother two's house. Brother A is on the other end of the line, and he says, "Today we race!" Here's the hint: Brother two says, "Oh no!" They go out to the track, and brother A beats the pistons off brother two.

How come?

#22

Puzzler Answer:

RAY: Why did brother two lose the race?

TOM: He lost the race because brother A waited until it was pouring rain, when brother two's car was in big trouble. Why? Slicks.

RAY: "Slicks" are tires without treads, so to speak, and they're not designed to run in wet weather.

TOM: The truth is, on flat dry roads—such as a racetrack—you get more traction without any tread, because all of the tire is directly in contact with the road. The only reason you have tread is to provide grooves for the water to escape. So in the rain, treads are great, but slicks are lousy.

RAY: Treads prevent a car from hydroplaning.

TOM: So brother A's car had a big advantage in the rain. Big enough to allow him to beat his smug younger brother.

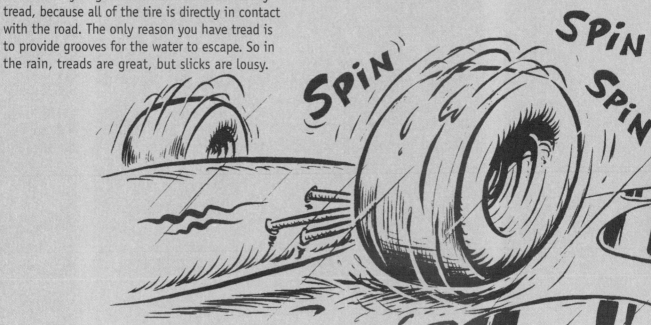

It Was a Dark and Stormy Night…

RAY: Let me set the scene for you. It was a dark and stormy night. Fred and his mother-in-law, Doris, are driving along in Fred's automobile.

TOM: Alone with his mother-in-law? This can't have a good ending.

RAY: There's a torrential downpour going on outside, and they come to a portion of the road that has been flooded out. Fred immediately comes to a halt in front of the huge puddle. Doris says, "What's the matter, Freddie?" He replies, "I can't go through this puddle. It looks like it's too deep. I know—let's sit here until we see another car go through. We'll see if he makes it. Then we'll decide what to do."

TOM: Got it. The American way. Let someone else go first!

RAY: So they wait and they wait. Did I tell you it's a dark and stormy night?

TOM: Why yes, I believe you mentioned that.

RAY: Seconds turn into minutes, minutes turn into hours. Days pass. Weeks, months (or at least it seems that way to Fred)! Finally another car approaches from the other direction. The car eases into the puddle. Fred and Doris can see that the water is well over the doorsills. Sure enough, however, the car slowly emerges from the puddle. Doris immediately chimes in: "I told you, Freddie, why don't you ever listen to me? I told you we can make it. Now let's get out of here!" Just as he's about to enter the puddle, however, Fred notices something about the other car that makes him stop dead in his tracks. He doesn't enter the puddle.

TOM: Was it a cement truck?

RAY: No, it is a sedan, and he notices something about it which causes him to stop immediately. He turns to Doris and proclaims, "We're doomed. Just because he made it doesn't mean that we will." What did Fred notice?

#23

Puzzler Answer:

TOM: As the car came out of the puddle and drove past him, Fred smelled diesel exhaust fumes. He remembered that diesel engines don't have ignition systems. So there were no spark-plug wires and no distributor cap to get wet.

RAY: Right. And if Fred had tried to go through, he knew, his wires and distributor would get wet, the car would stall, and he'd be stuck there in the middle of the puddle with his mother-in-law forever.

TOM: Oh, my God! I'm getting palpitations!

RAY: Calm down. It's just a puzzler.

The Gas Truck Puzzler

RAY: I remember when I was but a wee lad...

TOM: Yes, so do I.

RAY: Going for Sunday drives...going for Saturday drives...or going for any-day drives here in our fair city. On those drives, we would see large tanker trucks loaded with flammable materials like gasoline. These trucks would all have, hanging from their undercarriage, a large chain or other metal conductive contraption that went from the frame to the ground. The chain would throw off a shower of sparks as it dragged on the ground when the vehicle was in motion.

This puzzler is in the form of a two-part question. Part A: Why were those big tanker trucks dragging around chains in the old days?

TOM: And part B, I bet, is this: Why don't they have them anymore?

RAY: Right. And it's not due to the failure of the international chain crop last year.

#24

Puzzler Answer:

RAY: The answer, as it turns out, has nothing to do with that static charge that's built up when the vehicle is in motion. I used to think that those trucks had the chains in case they were struck by lightning, whereby the chain would be there to discharge the electricity into terra firma.

TOM: Grounded—just like our kids when they don't take out the garbage.

RAY: Precisely. But the real reason is this: When the tanker is dispensing its load, the flow of this flammable liquid through the hose will actually build up a charge, and the chain is there to dissipate *this* charge.

TOM: I don't believe you. Why doesn't it happen with my car?

RAY: What, do you deliver gas with your car?

TOM: So what's the answer to part B?

RAY: I'm getting to it, if you would just shut up for one minute. Nowadays there is a ground strap the delivery person hooks up when he puts the nozzle into the underground tank. This allows for the static to discharge while the fluid is flowing.

Puzzler 25

Faster than One of Mom's Dope Slaps

RAY: Here's a puzzler that was e-mailed to our Web site, the "Car Talk" section of cars.com. All I can deduce from the sender's e-mail address is that he is connected with OHSU.

TOM: What's OHSU?

RAY: Old Honolulu State University, I think. Anyway, his question is "What man-made object first broke the sound barrier?"

TOM: Wow! Are you going to give a hint?

RAY: I don't think so.

TOM: Was it the plane that Chuck Yeager flew in?

RAY: No.

TOM: That broke the sound barrier, didn't it?

RAY: Yes. But it was not the *first* man-made object to break the sound barrier. The object I'm thinking of predated Chuck Yeager.

TOM: Did it predate me?

RAY: Nothing predates you.

I just can't get over you, baby, so get up and turn off the light by yourself.

#25

Puzzler Answer:

TOM: I know the answer.

RAY: What is it?

TOM: The V-2 rocket. The year was 1942.

RAY: Sorry. The sound barrier was broken long, long before that, Tommy. Like, hundreds of years before that. The correct answer is "The common whip." The crack you hear is the tip of the whip breaking the sound barrier.

TOM: Actually, I thought the answer might have been one of mom's dope slaps. Those things come out of nowhere. I think she broke the sound barrier on at least several occasions.

RAY: Sound barrier? She broke the speed of light. You could never see that hand coming. Then all of a sudden, you'd feel it—*thwack!*—on the back of your head.

The Hirsute Hamlet

RAY: Imagine, if you will, a town in which there are 200,000 people.

TOM: Is it a fair city? Is that fair to say?

RAY: Yes, just like our fair city. Only, a little bigger. Here's what I want to know:

What are the chances that two inhabitants of that town have exactly the same number of hairs on their heads? I will stipulate that no one in this town has more than a 100,000 hairs.

TOM: And no one will have fewer than 1.

RAY: You know, you're not so dumb, are you now?

TOM: Now?

RAY: Never mind.

Ray tries to figure out how to charge a customer $800 for tightening his lug nuts.

#26

Puzzler Answer:

RAY: To answer this puzzler, you don't need to know anything about a branch of mathematics known as *combinatorial analysis* and the "Pigeonhole Principle."

TOM: But it might help you understand what's going on.

RAY: Distribute the first 100,000 people in such a way that no two people have the same number of hairs. In other words, you put each one of them in a little pigeonhole.

TOM: Like if you were to say, "How many hairs you got? One. Okay, you go in the one hole." The guy with two hairs goes in the number two hole, the next guy in the number three hole, and so on.

RAY: And if you have 100,000 people, you can get 100,000 different pigeonholes filled before anyone has to "share" a pigeonhole, right? But the very next person, the one hundred thousand-and-oneth person, must be a duplicate of one of the first 100,000. As a matter of fact, there are 100,000 people in this town who have the same number of hairs on their heads as the other people in town.

TOM: That's the most inane puzzler I've ever heard.

RAY: You can thank Martin Gardner for that one. I had nothing to do with it. I am officially distancing myself from this puzzler.

The Umpire and the Subway

RAY: A major-league umpire enters the subway by walking down the stairs with the assistance of his Seeing Eye dog.

TOM: You mean this ump is blind?!

RAY: Aren't they all? In fact, he had just come from Yankee Stadium where he was working behind the plate. Anyway, the dog leads him down to the subway platform where he arrives at a cage, behind which is sitting a woman.

TOM: The token vendor?

RAY: Yes. There is a sign below the window that says, "Tokens, 40 cents." The dog pees on the sign while the guys rummages around in his

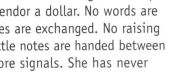

pocket. Through the slit in the cage, the ump hands the token vendor a dollar. No words are spoken. No gestures are exchanged. No raising of eyebrows. No little notes are handed between them. No semaphore signals. She has never seen him before.

TOM: But—has he ever seen her before?

RAY: No, you moron—he's blind. He's never seen anyone!

TOM: Oh, right!

RAY: Anyway, when she gets the dollar, she hands him two tokens and twenty cents change. Now, here's the question: How did she know he wanted two tokens and not one?

TOM: Is the dog involved?

RAY: The dog is not involved.

27

Puzzler Answer:

RAY: Here's how she knew. He did give her a dollar—but he didn't give her a dollar bill. He gave her four quarters.

TOM: So simple!

RAY: The blind guy gave the token vendor four quarters because he wanted two tokens. Otherwise, he would have given her two quarters.

TOM: For which he would have received one token and a dime change.

RAY: And if he had given her three quarters...

TOM: She would have given him a dope slap!

The Night Watchman

RAY: It was a dark and stormy night. A night watchman on duty in an old warehouse is making his rounds. He turns a corner in a hall. He walks down the hall. He stops. At the end of the hall is a door. Through the closed door he hears, "No, Frank, no, don't shoot! Don't shoot!"

TOM: Bang, bang!

RAY: What the hell was that?

TOM: I'm doing the sound effects.

RAY: The night watchman runs into the room. He opens the door. There's a doctor, a lawyer, and a plumber standing over the dead body. The gun is on the floor next to the dead body. He walks up to the plumber and he says, "You're under arrest for murder." How does he know it was the plumber?

TOM: No doctor or lawyer would be named Frank.

RAY: That's not the answer.

Ray and Tom teach Scott Simon to drive in NPR President Del Lewis's Mercedes.

#28

Puzzler Answer:

RAY: The night watchman knows that the plumber is the perpetrator—because the doctor and the lawyer were women.

TOM: And even though there could be a woman named Frank, I haven't met any. At least not any that I would want to date!

One Potato, Two Potato

RAY: Let's say, for the purpose of this puzzler, that potatoes are 99 percent water and 1 percent—what?

TOM: Potato.

RAY: Right.

TOM: Or, in honor of Dan Quayle, maybe we should make that "potatoe."

RAY: Okay. Now say you take 100 pounds of potatoes and you set them out on your back porch to dry out.

TOM: When they were completely dry, they would weigh 1 pound.

RAY: Right. Except, in this case, we don't want them to dry completely.

TOM: We don't?

RAY: No. We only want them to dry until the potatoes are 98 percent water.

TOM: Ah.

RAY: So the question is, how much will this pile of potatoes weigh when the potatoes are only 98 percent water?

TOM: Seems like a simple question.

RAY: I'll bet you get it wrong.

TOM: Well, you certainly have the odds in your favor on that bet.

#29

Puzzler Answer:

RAY: Do the math, Tommy!

TOM: Okay. When you have 1 part potato and 99 parts water, you have one 100 parts—and 99 percent of that is water.

RAY: Very good.

TOM: Now, to get down to 98 percent water, you need 2 parts potato for every 98 parts. That's the same as 1 part potato and... and... let me see... I'm still figuring...

RAY: Forty-nine parts water. That means there are 50 parts total, and one of those parts, or 2 percent, is potato.

TOM: So do you mean to tell me that when the potatoes are 98 percent water, they weigh only 50 pounds?

RAY: That's exactly right.

TOM: I love it. Does McDonald's know about this? And what about McDonald's customers? Do they know how much water they're getting with those fries? Someone should tell them! This is criminal, I tell you!

RAY: Forget the fries—how about the sodas?!

The Lost Marbles

RAY: This is an automotive puzzler. Imagine that you are sitting in the backseat of your car. You have three of those little felt bags with drawstrings that they use for jewelry.

TOM: Why are you in the backseat of your car?

RAY: I'm getting to that. Each one of these bags has ten marbles in it.

TOM: Let me guess. Are some of the marbles black and some of them white?

RAY: Yes.

TOM: I knew it. I knew it. Okay.

RAY: One of the bags has all white marbles. One bag has all black marbles. And one bag has half and half, five of each. Each of the bags has a label on it. However, every bag is labeled incorrectly.

TOM: Let me see if I have this right. One of the bags says "BLACK," one "WHITE," and one of the bags says "BOTH." And none of the labels is right.

RAY: Very good. Now, here are the rules: You can reach into any bag, draw out one marble, and look at it. The question is, what is the fewest number of bags you have to open to be able to put the labels on correctly?

TOM: Now tell me what the backseat of the car has to do with this.

RAY: Nothing. That just made it an automotive puzzler.

Puzzler Answer:

RAY: What is the minimum number of bags you must reach into in order to label the bags correctly? One.

TOM: Huh?

RAY: One. To understand the solution to this puzzler, you have to use the fact that all of the bags start out incorrectly labeled. Do you remember that?

TOM: I remember.

RAY: So you would start by reaching into the bag labeled "BOTH"—the one that's supposed to have both black and white marbles. You pull a marble out of that bag, and you see what color it is. Now you know it doesn't have the black-and-white mixture in there, because I told you that all of the bags were labeled incorrectly. So when you pull out a marble from that bag, you know the bag contains all marbles of that color.

TOM: Right. So you pull out a white marble. You know that's the bag of white marbles.

RAY: Right. So you find the bag that says "WHITE," and you swap labels with the one that says "BOTH."

TOM: I think I'm still with you.

RAY: Now, you know that the bag that says, "WHITE" is correctly labeled, right? The only question is, what about the other two?

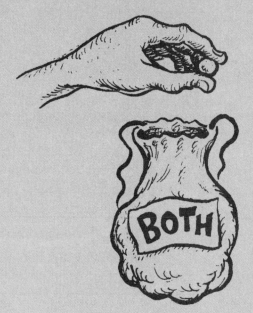

#30

TOM: Yeah. What about the other two?

RAY: Well, you remember that all of the bags were labeled incorrectly at the start. Now you know that...

—The "WHITE" bag is now labeled correctly.

—But the "BLACK" bag still has its original label, which you know must be incorrect. So you must do what?

TOM: Switch the labels on the last two bags. Wow.

RAY: Elegant, isn't it?

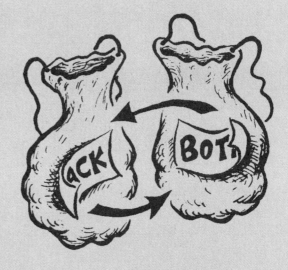

Latin Scholar Word Derivation

TOM: As you know, I'm into derivations of words. And, as you also know, I am a Latin scholar, having won the Latin prize when I was in kindergarten. According to my mother.

RAY: Sounds like bull stercus to me!

TOM: Back in Roman times, it was said that all roads led to Rome. And, in fact, some of these roads which led to Rome intersected. On some occasions, there were places where not only two roads intersected, but even three roads intersected.

RAY: Got it.

TOM: Now, are you ready for this?

RAY: I've been ready for the last half hour.

TOM: It was a practice (this is a *big hint* here) that where three roads met, people would often stop to chat. They would talk about things, and even leave messages for their friends, and various notes and items of interest. Travelers would chisel the notes up on the little stone pillars—*stelae,* as they were referred to in the Sunday *Roman Times* crossword puzzle. Now the question.

RAY: Oh, I thought the question was "Are you still awake?"

TOM: The question is this: An interesting English word derives from this little story. What's the word?

RAY: Gee, this is historic.

TOM: Historic and folkloric.

RAY: And poorly crafted.

TOM: But somewhat interesting?

RAY: Yes, somewhat interesting.

#31

Puzzler Answer:

RAY: How would you say in Latin, "Three roads"?

TOM: I would say it thusly: *Tres viae*.

RAY: Very good. *T-R-E-S V-I-A-E*. Right?

TOM: But of course in English, when we say three, the prefix is *tri,* T-R-I.

RAY: Like a *tri*-cornered hat.

TOM: Like a *tri*pod.

RAY: Or tri-*this*.

TOM: And *via* means singular road. Although we left off the "e."

RAY: Because we're what? Illiterates.

TOM: And we came up with the word *tri-via*. "Trivia," which is the little messages and notes and odds and ends that were left for other travelers. So where the three roads met, the little notes that were left there became "trivia."

Bizarre British Travel Habits

RAY: Back many years ago, the Brits had colonized, among other places, India.

TOM: Those stinkin' Brits colonized the whole world!

RAY: And to get to India, traveling by boat was the preferred method of transportation for the British upper crust.

TOM: British Airways had not been invented yet.

RAY: Very good. When India-bound travelers went to get their tickets, if they were sufficiently wealthy, they would ask the ticketing agent for specific accommodations. On the way out—to India—they would ask for a state room on the port, or left, side of the ship. On the trip home to merry old England, they would ask for accommodations on the starboard, or right, side of the ship.

TOM: Those Brits are wacko, aren't they?

RAY: We'll leave it to you to figure out why they wanted to travel in this fashion. However, out of this peculiar travel, a word was invented.

TOM: Was it "blimey"?

RAY: I don't think so.

#32

Puzzler Answer:

RAY: The word is "posh."

TOM: And it stood for "Port Out, Starboard Home."

RAY: Pretty good, huh?

TOM: Very good.

RAY: Imagine for a moment that you're sailing from England to India. The hot afternoon sun would be on the right-hand side of the ship as you sail all the way down the west coast of Africa, which is the longest leg of the trip.

TOM: Forget that. I'd want to be on the other side of the ship.

RAY: Exactly. And on the return trip, you'd want the sun in some other jerk's room. If you were traveling P.O.S.H., you'd be on the starboard side of the ship coming home.

TOM: The ship didn't go in reverse to get back to England?

RAY: I don't think so.

The Heisenberg Principle and the Chicken Truck

RAY: Here's a classic "chicken" puzzler that has been passed down through the ages.

TOM: Yeah. I think it originated with Frank Perdusius and the ancient Greeks.

RAY: Anyway, there's a chicken rancher carrying 1,000 pounds of chickens in a truck that weighs 2 tons. That means that when he's carrying the chickens, the total weight of the truck is what?

TOM: Five thousand pounds. Is this guy a boneless-chicken rancher?

RAY: I don't know. I've never seen his X rays. He's driving along, when he comes to a bridge with a warning sign that says: "Maximum Weight: 5,000 Pounds." Now, weighing 350 himself, he figures he'll just jump out and everything will be fine. But he realizes that, even right at the 5,000-pound limit, the bridge might collapse.

TOM: He's right on the feathery edge, so to speak.

RAY: Suddenly, however, he has a brilliant idea— or so he thinks. He decides he'll get all these birds flapping their wings and up in the air...not standing in the truck.

TOM: How's he going to do that?

RAY: He's going to get out of the truck, whack the sides of the truck, and squeeze off a few rounds with his forty-five.

TOM: I get it. The idea is that as long as the chickens are flying and not sitting in the truck, the truck will revert to its base weight of 4,000 pounds, right?

RAY: That's if he can get all of them in the air. But even if he gets 50 percent of them in the air at any time—

TOM: That's good enough.

RAY: So the question is: Does he make it? And: Why doesn't he make it?

#33

Puzzler Answer:

RAY: He doesn't make it, because the downward air pressure exerted by the wings of the chickens is at least equivalent to the weight of the chickens. Otherwise, how would the chickens fly?

TOM: So this is the basic principle of flight?

RAY: No, it's the principle of enclosed chicken trucks. Those chickens have to exert a downward pressure on the column of air between them and the truck. And that pressure has to at least equal their weight. That force is ultimately being exerted on the truck...and the bridge...and that's the driver's undoing. *Q.E.D.*

TOM: But, wait a minute. I have another question for you. What if the truck was really tall—like a mile tall—and the chickens were flapping their wings, way up at the top of the truck?

RAY: Well, then you'd make it over the bridge, but you'd never make it under the next highway crossing.

Editor's Note: This answer is only correct if the truck is closed and hermetically sealed (in which case banging on the side of the truck would be useless because the chickens would probably be dead anyway).

How many turkeys can you find in this picture?

Mark the Shark

RAY: This puzzler comes to me via our esteemed producer Doug Berman and Mark the Shark, our crack bookkeeper at Dewey, Cheetham & Howe.

TOM: Is he the guy who keeps both sets of books?

RAY: That's the guy. Anyway, it was the end of the month, and Mark and Dougie were attempting to balance the books. Mark was looking over the bank statement. Dougie, meanwhile, had the calculator and was adding up a long list of numbers from the checkbook. Mark says, "Okay, Dougie, what did you come up with?" To which Dougie replies, "I came up with..." and he mumbles a depressingly small number. Mark says, "Wrong number." And Doug says, *"Doh!"*

TOM: So you mean to say our checkbook doesn't match with the bank statement?

RAY: Exactly. So Dougie says, "Oh man, you mean I'm going to have to add this whole page of numbers all over again?" To which Mark replies, "Well, wait a minute, how much are we off by?" And Dougie says, "Twenty-seven cents." Mark ponders the significance of this number for a few moments, and then proclaims, "You don't have to add that whole column of numbers again. I know what you did wrong."

TOM: No wonder they call him "Mark the Shark."

RAY: That isn't why.

TOM: I didn't think so.

RAY: Mark says, "You transposed two numbers."

TOM: How did he know that?

RAY: That's the question. Sure enough, Dougie goes back and looks at the printout from the calculator—and Mark was right. He had transposed two numbers. Where there was supposed to be a seventy-four, he had punched in forty-seven.

TOM: And he found it just like that?

RAY: Just like that.

TOM: Thanks to Mark "the Shark."

RAY: What did Mark know that Dougie didn't know?

TOM: Geez! The answer to that could fill whole libraries.

RAY: You're right. Let me phrase it another way: In this particular case, what did Mark know— that Dougie didn't?

#34

Puzzler Answer:

TOM: Here's a little math secret: If you're adding up a column of numbers and you transpose two numbers, the difference between the wrong sum and the correct sum will always be a multiple of nine.

RAY: Twenty-seven was a multiple of nine.

TOM: It still is.

RAY: So Mark knew it was a "transpositional error." Here, I'll show you:

TOM: One of Mark the Shark's many accountant's tricks?

RAY: This is one of the ones that the IRS *does* know about.

TOM: Right. And one which they don't mind. Do they care about bank accounts in the Cayman Islands?

RAY: Quiet!

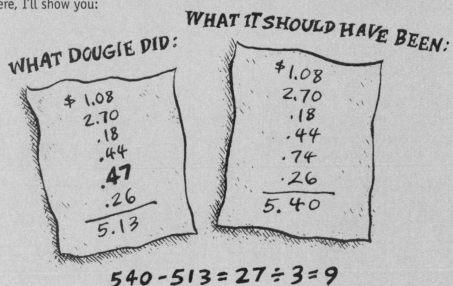

WHAT DOUGIE DID:

$1.08
2.70
.18
.44
.47
.26
_____
5.13

WHAT IT SHOULD HAVE BEEN:

$1.08
2.70
.18
.44
.74
.26
_____
5.40

$$540 - 513 = 27 \div 3 = 9$$

Ray takes the final exam in his correspondence school dentistry course.

Why "Wood" They Use Poplar?

RAY: Some years ago, my wife and I took a trip south; I can't remember what our final destination was.

TOM: Was it South Boston?

RAY: No, actually it was West Virginia. I got the notion that I wanted to explore some abandoned mines. So I engaged a guide.

TOM: Guido the guide?

RAY: No, Lefty. He used to run alligator-sightseeing tours in the Everglades, shuttling tourists around in one of those fan-powered boat. But after the accident, he couldn't work the boat controls with only one arm, so...

TOM: Ah. Gotcha.

RAY: Now, the only image I have of mines is from those old Westerns where the mines—the walls and the roofs of the mines—were shored up with timbers.

TOM: Volvo used to do that.

RAY: That's right. I was surprised to find out that they still shore up the walls of the mines with timbers. And being somewhat of a wood connoisseur, I asked Lefty what kind of wood it was because I didn't recognize it.

TOM: Let me guess. He said, "Hey pal, as far as I'm concerned, you seen one tree, you've seen 'em all."

RAY: No, he didn't, you yahoo. Anyway, I looked at a few other mines and they all had the same kind of wood. I would have thought that in that neck of the woods, they would have used something like oak or ash, which are very strong woods. But neither of these woods was used. Someone told me they used a wood called poplar or tulip poplar and I said, "Gee, that's kind of unusual. That can't be anywhere near as strong as a big piece of oak or ash. There had to be some reason."

TOM: So what's the reason?

RAY: That's the question. Why do they use poplar? It's not because it happens to be growing twenty feet away from the mine entrance, either.

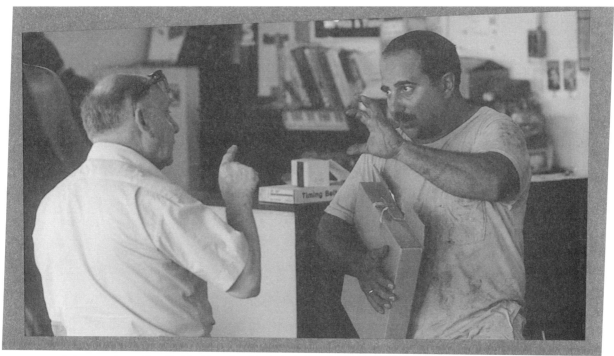

Ray reacts calmly as customer Ben Kachinski again objects to being charged $1,500 for an oil change.

#35

Puzzler Answer:

TOM: Can I take a crack at it? I have no idea what the answer is.

RAY: Well, in your own inimitable way of being unencumbered by the thought process, you came very close when you said, "Can I take a crack at it."

TOM: Huh?

RAY: It so happens that when the poplar begins to buckle from the weight of the coal or the diamonds, or the earth, or whatever is above, it cracks. But, it doesn't just crack. It cracks with a very loud noise. Many stronger woods make no noise when they're about to give out.

TOM: Sonia Henie's tutu!

RAY: But poplar has the interesting characteristic that when it's getting ready to give, it begins to emit loud cracking noises in advance of the actual failure. These noises, if you listen very carefully—

TOM: Let me guess. If you played the tape backwards, very slowly, it would sound like, "Run! Run! The sky is falling!"

Puzzler 36

Algebra Under the Big Tent

RAY: Ready for a mathematical puzzler?

TOM: Am I ever! Avogadro's number, Fermat's theorem, you name it. I'm ready!

RAY: Okay. One hundred people attend a circus, and the total admissions come to exactly $100.

TOM: Got it. They pay a buck a piece.

RAY: No, that would be too easy. That was "Romper Room"'s puzzler last week. Ours is a little trickier.

TOM: It's never that easy, is it?

RAY: No. The admission charges in our puzzler are actually $5 per man, $2 per woman—

TOM: Isn't that kind of sexist?

RAY: And the admission per child is 10 cents.

TOM: A little ageist, wouldn't you say?

RAY: The question is, how many men, women, and children attended?

#36

Puzzler Answer:

RAY: "Piece of cake, guys!" you say. And you might start by writing down your equations: $x+y+z$, with x being men, y being women, z being children. Then you have $5x+2y+.1z=\$100$. And $x+y+z=100$ people. So you solve for x, y, or z...but you soon come to realize that you have two equations—but three unknowns.

TOM: This is not as simple as it looks. You might think it's a simple algebraic problem, but it's not. You can't solve for three variables with just two equations. So the trick to solving this problem is guesswork.

RAY: Ah! Kind of like on our show.

TOM: Right. This requires some trial and error.

RAY: We know that we have to end up with a nice round $100 in admissions.

TOM: Yeah, so what?

RAY: So we know that the children must come in increments of 10. Otherwise, you'd come up with an admissions amount of, like, $97.60. Right?

TOM: Ah! Of course! So that narrows it down a lot.

RAY: So then you start your trial-and-error calculations. You start by assuming there are 10 kids. Ten kids give you a buck in admissions. You can then solve for adults, and your first equation would be $5x+2y=99$. And $x+y=90$.

TOM: So you keep trying to solve for x and y with different numbers of kids—10 kids, 20 kids, and so on. With 20 kids,

If there are 10 kids at 10¢ apiece, then:

$$5x+2y=99$$
$$x+y=90$$
$$x=90-y$$
$$So. . .$$
$$5(90-y)+2y=99$$
$$450-5y+2y=99$$
$$35y=3y$$
$$117=y$$

Wrong answer, substitute a different multiple of 10 for the number of kids.

#36

your equations are $5x+2y=98$, and $x+y=80$. And you solve that one and it doesn't work either until finally, you try to solve the equation with 70 kids—that is, $x+y=30$, and $5x+2y=93$—and you come up with the answer.

RAY: Nineteen women, 11 men, and 70 kids. *Q.E.D.*

In the Hot Seat with Larry D'Onofrio

RAY: The other day I was test-driving a customer's car, and I ran into a buddy of mine, Larry D'Onofrio.

TOM: Did you hit him hard?

RAY: Not that hard, but they called the ambulance anyway. Larry tells me, "I was eagerly awaiting the return of the puzzler from its puzzler summer hiatus. I've been listening for years, and I'm always intimidated by the puzzler. I've never gotten the right answer. So imagine my disappointment when the premiere puzzler of the season was about 'toilet sweat.' " *[Editor's note: The "Toilet Sweat" puzzler did not make the cut for this book. See Volume II.]* He says, "'I never thought I'd be able to help you with a puzzler, but, Ray, I've got one that's a heck of a lot better than that one." "Proceed," I say. Larry goes on:

"When I was in college, I had a VW Beetle. I was mechanically uninclined." Meaning, what?

TOM: He was a klutz.

RAY: Exactly. But, Larry says, he was encouraged by the John Muir book—you know, the VW book for the complete idiot. He said he was amazed by the number of things he was able to do, and the number of things he could fix over the years that he had his VW. For example, he was even able to repair the clutch. One summer evening, however, Larry made a repair that involved something as simple as loosening a few bolts, replacing something, and then tightening up the bolts. He said, "It was that simple." Larry continued, "There were three bolts that I loosened, and three bolts that I tightened—and everything else was fine. The car ran just great for weeks. I returned to school in the fall, and a couple of buddies and I decided to go out one night to scoop some babes."

TOM: Yeah, sure, good luck. Four guys in a Beetle.

RAY: So Larry says that the four of them pile into the VW, and are on their way to their favorite watering hole...when suddenly the car bursts into flames.

TOM: You got a problem with that?

RAY: The question, very simply, is this: What repair did Larry do that enabled the car to run for six weeks...and then suddenly burst into flames?

TOM: This is good! Very good!

Exhibit A, Consumer Protection Agency: Case #134B, Ray Magliozzi versus the Commonwealth of Massachusetts.

#37

Puzzler Answer:

RAY: Now, there are many repairs that Larry could have done that might have caused the car to burst into flames after a few weeks. For example, he could have replaced the fuel pump and not have tightened the nuts.

TOM: Sure.

RAY: But I gave you a hint. Larry's VW didn't self-immolate until he piled into it with all of his buddies.

TOM: Yeah, so?

RAY: What he had done was to install a new battery. And, if you remember, the batteries in VW bugs were located under the backseat.

TOM: Right! And if you're going to take all those guys in a VW, you've got to use the backseat. And I bet one of his roommates was large-butted, right?

RAY: "Lard Butt," you might say. Lard Butt sat down on the seat, and the seat had...what?

TOM: Coils. Metal coils.

RAY: Right. Metal coil springs underneath, which were covered with a strawlike material.

TOM: Kapok. Or jute. Or maybe bubble gum wrappers.

RAY: There you go. It was straw. And, of course, the terminals on the battery were too tall. Larry had installed the wrong battery. So as soon as Lard Butt sat down, those springs made contact with the positive and negative terminals of the battery. That short-circuited the battery and set the seat on fire.

TOM: Pretty funny!

RAY: You bet! Larry said, "You never saw four guys move faster in your life!" You know what else was funny?

#37

TOM: Their butts were on fire?

RAY: Exactly.

TOM: But, you know, you have to wonder how long that one guy, who was sitting directly over the battery, sat there before he realized that his butt was on fire! Now, that's funny!

Supermarket Skid Saver

RAY: It's winter. A fellow takes his wife shopping at the convenience store. She says, "I'll be right out, hon. I just have to run in and pick up a few things." So as soon as she leaves, he lights a cigar, turns on the game, and puts the seat in the fully reclined position.

RAY: Some minutes later, his wife comes out of the store with a bag full of items. She gets in the car, he starts the car up, and he tries to pull away when he realizes...he's stuck on the ice. The wheels are spinning—they're going *woo woo woo woo woo*. His wife says, "Wait a minute, hon. I have something in the bag here that I believe will get you out of this fix."

TOM: "Really?" he says. "A fifty-pound bag of sand?"

RAY: "No."

TOM: "Blowtorch?"

RAY: "No," she says, as she starts pulling stuff out of the bag. "Here's what I have...
• a bottle of Filippo Berio extra virgin olive oil,
• a family-size tube of Preparation H™,
• a jar of chunky peanut butter,
• a gallon of chlorine bleach,
• a head of iceberg lettuce,
• a pound of kielbasa, and
• a spray can of Cheez Whiz™."

TOM: Intimate little dinner tonight, huh?

RAY: Which one of these items is most likely to help them get off the ice?

Tom and Ray organize the fruit pickers in Fredonia, 1969

#38

Puzzler Answer:

RAY: What do you think? You don't have a thought, do you?

TOM: Almost every one of those items might help get them off the ice, except for the extra virgin olive oil.

RAY: But which is the one that is most likely to help? You don't have a clue, do you? The answer is: the chlorine bleach.

TOM: You don't say.

RAY: I do say.

TOM: You do?

RAY: Chlorine bleach, if poured on the rubber, will soften it enough to make it more sticky, so that it will create a greater coefficient of friction between the tire and the ice. Just to prove this to myself, I went over to our producer Dougie Berman's house and I poured chlorine bleach all over his Miata. I started right from the roof and let it drip down onto the tires. It worked like a charm—all four tires are stuck right to the pavement.

TOM: Well, that's probably true, because chlorine bleach, also known as sodium hypochlorite, does have a reaction with rubber.

RAY: We should point out, however, that this may also ruin the tire, so I wouldn't try this little approach in a non-puzzler-book environment. In a real-world situation, I'd try the peanut butter.

Earth, Air, Fire, and Water

RAY: A customer has his car towed into a repair shop because it won't run. He gets into the car and turns the key. The car cranks, *ruh-ruh-ruh. Ruh-ruh-ruh. Ruh-ruh-ruh-ruh-ruh-ruh-ruh. Ruh-ruh-ruh. Ruh-ruh-ruh.*
Ruh-ruh-ruh-ruh-ruh-ruh-ruh. Ruh-ruh-ruh. Ruh-ruh-ruh. Ruh-ruh-ruh-ruh-ruh-ruh-ruh.
Ruh-ruh-ruh. Ruh-ruh-ruh. Ruh-ruh-ruh-ruh-ruh-ruh. Ruh-ruh-ruh. Ruh-ruh-ruh.
Ruh-ruh-ruh-ruh-ruh-ruh. Ruh-ruh-ruh. Ruh-ruh-ruh. Ruh-ruh-ruh-ruh-ruh-ruh-ruh.

TOM: Alright, alright! Stop! We get the idea.

RAY: It may fire up for a second or two, but it won't keep running. So the mechanic says, "I'll have to check it for spark."

TOM: So he checks for spark. Does he have a spark?

RAY: Yes. He checks for gas. It has gas. In fact, this car has something called "throttle body fuel injection," so it's easy to see if the engine is getting gas. When you crank the engine, he sees gas pouring in, just like a carburetor.

TOM: So you're telling me, this guy has spark and he has fuel. What more does he want?

RAY: Air. And he has that. Air's all around us, right? Of course he's got air. Otherwise, this puzzler would have taken place in the orbit surrounding Uranus.

TOM: I beg your pardon? Anyway, so it appears that he has all the necessary ingredients for combustion. And yet the car won't run. So what does he do next?

RAY: He takes out one of the spark plugs. I don't know why he does this, but he takes one of them out.

TOM: And?

RAY: The engine starts, and continues to run. On three cylinders, no less!

TOM: What, pray tell, prompted him to do this?

RAY: I don't know! But the question is: Why did removing the spark plug allow this guy's car to start?

Doug drives Tom and Ray to work.

146 a Haircut in Horse Town...

Puzzler Answer:

RAY: The ingredient he was missing...exhaust!

TOM: Hold on just a minute. Exhaust is not one of the ingredients for combustion, is it?

RAY: Oh, but it is. It's a little-known fact. Ponds and Fleischmann discovered this in the laboratory. In order for the engine to work, it must get rid of its exhaust.

TOM: Of course. If you can't get exhaust out of the cylinders, there's no room for fresh air and the gasoline to come in. So the car won't run. And this guy had a plugged-up exhaust system. His neighbor was miffed at him, and stuck a potato in his tailpipe.

RAY: Exactly. Or he had a plugged-up catalytic converter. And when he took out one of the spark plugs, he allowed the exhaust to sneak out through that cylinder.

RAY: Right. In other words, that open cylinder was acting like the exhaust pipe. The exhaust that should have been going out the tailpipe came out that spark-plug hole instead.

TOM: The engine ran loudly, but it ran. I like it!

Old Skin Flint's Fuel

RAY: I'm going to recite a conversation to you that took place a long time ago.

TOM: Was King Tutankhamen involved?

RAY: I don't think so. Here are the excerpts. Your job is to tell me what they're talking about: "Boy, it was a great machine, and the Ford dealer sold me the deluxe model for only a dollar more." Later on in the conversation was heard, "...And I would often stop by the Ford dealership where I would buy the fuel for only 5 cents a pound."

TOM: Wow!

RAY: What are they talking about?

TOM: What are they talking about?

RAY: Is there an echo in here? Here's a hint: You couldn't get this at a Chevrolet dealer or a Buick dealer.

#40

Puzzler Answer:

RAY: For only 5 cents a pound, what were they talking about?

TOM: I still don't know what it was.

RAY: Well, as you know very well, Henry Ford was a cheapskate, right?

TOM: Of course. He was known for that.

RAY: "Old Skin Flint," I think they called him. Well, it turns out that Henry used to have a lumber operation where they made wood panels for the station wagons. Being the cheapskate that he was, Henry hated to see scrap wood go to waste, so he would take the leftovers and he would have them made into charcoal briquettes.

TOM: I knew that. Heck, I think I bought some briquettes from the man.

RAY: To assure that there would be customers for the briquettes, he had backyard charcoal grills made up and Henry forced the Ford dealers to sell them. It cost $2 for the cheapo grill and 3 bucks for the deluxe model.

TOM: Which must have had the rotating spit?

RAY: Interestingly, this lasted until the mid-'40s, when the plant closed down. The manager of that plant, who later went on to briquette fame, was a fellow named Kingsford.

TOM: That's a bold-faced lie. His name was Weber.

The Symbol of Agincourt

RAY: It was a dark and stormy night, October 1415. The scene: Agincourt, France. Earlier that year, Henry V of England had invaded France because he thought he was an heir to the French throne. Now, these were the good old days when a king actually went to fight with his soldiers. You know, they lost a lot of kings before they figured out it might be wiser to keep the kings at home and let the knights do all the fighting.

TOM: I beg to differ! I like the old way better. If the king wants to go to war, he should get out there and fight. This is how it should be done—even now. "Mr. President, here are your fatigues. Now, get in the damn jeep!"

RAY: Anyway, after spending many months there, Henry, being unsuccessful at taking over France, decides to pack his bags and head back to England. Besides, the Brits were all hungry, they had been weakened by disease—and they were in dire need of fish and chips.

TOM: I bet they were fed up with those damn French, too!

RAY: They couldn't stand the French. So they decided to go to Calais where they were going to hitch a boat ride to merry old England.

TOM: How are you going to turn this into a puzzler?

RAY: I'm working on it...Henry V tries to sue for peace. He says, "I'm tired. I'm sick. I want to go home. I don't want to fight." The French say, "Tough. You're fighting." Now, the French are led by a guy named D'Albret, who has a force of about 25,000. Henry V, on the other hand, has got about 6,000 tired guys. The French are convinced that the Brits are done for.

TOM: Sure, they've got them outnumbered 12 to 1!

Tom and Harriet spend another cozy night in the garage—on orders from the head of the household.

RAY: Right. Whatever you say. So the French prepare for battle. They proclaim that when the battle is over, they will take the British soldiers that have not been killed and remove certain parts of their bodies so that they might never be able to fight again.

TOM: What?!

RAY: No, you sicko—not *those* parts. *Other* parts. Well, it turns out that the battle was preceded by heavy rains and the French were at a disadvantage. They were in a valley and were weighted down by their heavy armor. Plus the tactics of the British soldiers were superior. And, get this—the Brits won!

TOM: No kidding?

RAY: They did indeed. They won in a decisive battle. In fact, D'Albret and several of his dukes and counts and about 500 other members of the French nobility were killed in the battle. Needless to say, there were no parts of anyone's body cut off by the French army. And just to taunt the French when the battle was over, the victorious British displayed what was to have been cut off, as a symbol of derision toward their would-be conquerors.

TOM: Was this the origin of the expression "Nyah-na-na-na-na?"

RAY: What were they brandishing? It is a popular symbol, known to this day by most adults and some children.

TOM: Wow.

#41

Puzzler Answer:

RAY: What I didn't mention was that the British were archers. While the French were stuck in their little valley, the small group of British soldiers were able to overwhelm them. The French were bogged down in the mud, but the British were shooting arrows from atop the hill.

TOM: And arrows go fast downhill!

RAY: They certainly do. Now the British knew that—

TOM: Heck, even my Dodge Dart goes fast downhill!

RAY: Let's not get carried away, Tommy. The French knew that many of the British soldiers were archers, so they had threatened to cut off the fingers that the British used to pull back the bowstring.

TOM: The index and middle finger of the right hand.

RAY: And by holding up those two fingers, thus was born the "V for Victory" sign.

TOM: I thought that Richard Nixon invented that sign.

Editor's Note: Several people suggested that it was the middle finger only, but since this is a family book, we opted for the two-finger answer.

What?
You think this book is going to go on forever?

You think puzzlers grow on trees? Actually, we have about ten more good ones, but we're saving them for *Great Car Talk Puzzlers Volume II*, tentatively due out in the spring of 2023 (if we stay on our tight schedule). Seriously, thank you very much for reading our little book. And thanks for supporting Car Talk and your favorite NPR station. If you should find yourself in desperate need of more copies of this fine work of literature (if you want to send one to a friend, need to start a bonfire, or have a wobbly coffee table that needs to be leveled), you can get additional copies by calling 1-888-CAR-JUNK. Have somebody else's credit card ready.

Acknowledgments

Without the help of the following individuals, this book probably would not have come out until the year 2168: Car Talk interns Shay Zeller, Delaney Smith, and Bill Jacobs...Alison Herschberg, Andy Mayer, Simon Sung, and Lissa Wolfendale at becker&mayer!...Car Talk Plaza's Doug Mayer, Ken Rogers, Catherine Ray, and Zuzu....Robert Auman, John Burke, and Janice Gavin at VisAbility, and official DCH staff photographer Richie Howard.

INDEX